THE ＇
OF NE

Tony Higgott

COUNTRYSIDE BOOKS
NEWBURY, BERKSHIRE

First published 2001
© Tony Higgott 2001

COUNTRYSIDE BOOKS
3 Catherine Road
Newbury, Berkshire

ISBN 1 85306 718 0

To view our complete range of books,
please visit us at
www.countrysidebooks.co.uk

Cover illustration: The Old Granaries – a watercolour
by Victor M. Corden c 1910

Produced through MRM Associates Ltd., Reading
Typeset by Techniset Typesetters, Newton-le-Willows
Printed by Borcombe Printers, Romsey

CONTENTS

ACKNOWLEDGEMENTS

The idea for a simple, readable history of Newbury came about in the 1970s as a result of the popularity of the former Borough Council Guide, whose text had been written by local historian R. Neville Hadcock. A book with Hadcock's basic text duly appeared in 1979 as *The Story of Newbury*, published by Countryside Books. This was later revised by Cecilia Millson with help from others. The chapter relating the events of the 17th century Civil War in Newbury was written by Derek Carruthers for that edition and is retained here.

This new history of the town carries the same title and contains many sections from the earlier book, but much new information has been added. In particular, the twentieth century and architectural heritage sections have been completely rewritten and expanded.

The publishers are grateful to photographers and others who have provided illustrations for the book, especially Peter Bloodworth Photography, EC Paine Ltd and the *Newbury Weekly News*, where Margaret Carruthers was particularly helpful. They are especially grateful to Mrs Sue Hopson who has made images available from her collection of historic postcards and to West Berkshire Heritage Service who also have allowed some of their pictures of the town in the past to be included. The author also thanks the Heritage Service, especially Paul Cannon, for help with tracing sources of information. Many commercial firms assisted by providing information about their current and past business in Newbury, not all of which it has been appropriate to include in this brief account. These include: David Wilson Homes (re Trencherwood) – John Wells; Kerridge Computers – Steve Johnson; Kleinwort Benson – Peter Churchill-Coleman; Merant (re Micro Focus) – Joan Vincent; Nextra (re Norsk Data) – Hazel Crispin; Opperman Mastergear – Jo Page; Quantel – Roger Thornton; UK Solenoid – Rowland Bartlett; Vodafone – Ally Major. The following people kindly provided information on sports: hot-air ballooning – Pete Bish; Newbury and Crookham Golf Club – Brian Bowness; Newbury Rugby Football Club – Chet Hobbs and for Royal Berkshire Fire & Rescue Service – Wendy Ross.

To all these and others who have given invaluable help, the publishers would like to record their appreciation and thanks.

INTRODUCTION

Newbury is situated on a bridging point of the River Kennet, the main tributary of the Thames. It is halfway between London and Bath at the crossing of main routes from east to west, and from the Midlands to the south coast. This central position not only made the town popular with medieval traders and of strategic importance to the opposing forces in the Civil War, but has proved attractive to today's leading business people.

There has been rapid growth of the town and its surrounding villages since the Second World War. In the past much of the town's commercial activity was connected to agriculture, but as suppliers of seeds, fertilisers, equipment etc and buyers of animals or produce have become much bigger in scale, operating from distant centres, so that connection has been lost. Obviously, the banks, solicitors and estate managing companies continue to do business with the farming community, but their business is not as obvious as a truck load of cattle or grain. However, the two day Newbury Agricultural Show at its showground at Chieveley continues to attract thousands of local people each year, although even that has lost some of its purely agricultural interest to shopping and spectacle. Different employment opportunities have been provided by the new businesses – some are major world companies – which now operate from the town. However, Newbury's markets are still held twice weekly, and provide a link with its past, for it was founded as a trading centre with a market over nine hundred years ago.

The town is situated 77 metres (250 ft) above sea level and set in the Kennet Valley, flanked by the heathland plateaux of Snelsmore, Cold Ash, Greenham and Wash Common. A little further north or south finds the chalk downlands of Berkshire/Oxfordshire or Hampshire, with Walbury Hill, near Inkpen, the highest point in southern England.

Set in the heart of the countryside, yet within easy reach of London and the south coast, this is a favoured residential area and popular with commuters. Whilst not a holiday resort the town is becoming a recognised centre for short breaks and for touring. It has also been growing as a place where tourists stay after arriving at (or before leaving from) Heathrow or the south coast ports. Its position makes it ideal for reaching some of the most historic, interesting and beautiful places in this part of Britain.

—————————CHAPTER ONE—————————
The Early History

The first written record of people living in the Newbury area comes in the late Saxon period, apart from brief references from the time when the Romans occupied most of Britain. All the information we have from the long period before history begins is learnt from the archaeological record; the tangible objects and structures which have survived from the past. The archaeological record, like the historical one, is selective and incomplete. Some materials, stone, pottery and certain metals, survive quite well whilst others such as wood, bone and leather do not survive for as long. Additionally, poor people had very little in the way of possessions, many items are destroyed during the lifetime of the owner and in any case there must be much material still waiting to be recovered.

The earliest evidence of man to be found in the Newbury area is the crude flint tools, mainly hand-axes, used by Neanderthal Man during the Old Stone Age, around 250 thousand years ago. In the past these were frequently found in the gravelly soils which cover the higher ground such as Wash Common and the gravels of the Kennet Valley. People still occasionally come across examples when digging their gardens.

No evidence has yet been found in this area of the places inhabited by these people. This is not surprising as they were living before the peak of the last Ice Age. Although glaciers did not cover Britain as far south as the Newbury area the ground here would have been permanently frozen and tundra-like in the warmer spells. However, when the ice-cap finally began to melt and recede, the whole area would have been affected by the resulting floodwaters. It was at this time that the course of the River Thames changed to something like that which it follows today and when the valley of the River Kennet, like other southern rivers, was cut to its present depth. The floodwaters swept away surface material and, as the torrents slowed, first deposited the heavier material whilst carrying the lighter sediments further. This resulted in the thick layer of gravel in the Kennet and Thames Valleys which is being extracted today.

Towards the end of this period, as the climate improved, people again began to use this area. The tools they used are of a different form and these people were direct ancestors of modern man. An important site from this era was discovered around 1960 at Crown Acres, to the south-west of Thatcham and dug away by gravel extraction. Material from the site is preserved at West Berkshire Museum.

Other finds of the Ice Age period from the Newbury-Thatcham area are tusks and molars of mammoth, and antlers of red deer. From a much warmer period, before the Ice Age reached its peak, are bones of a hippopotamus, found at Shaw when the present A339 was being built.

When the extremes of the Ice Age finally came to an end conditions improved rapidly and there is evidence of people in the Kennet Valley at this time. Presumably animals returned first followed by man who was still leading a nomadic way of life, hunting animals and gathering other food, such as fruit, nuts and roots, where it could be found. As Britain was still joined by land to mainland Europe at the beginning of this period, the Middle Stone Age or Mesolithic, it would be relatively easy for people to get here.

Basically it is only stone tools which survive from this period, but the techniques of manufacture and the range of types are much developed. The tools are mainly based on carefully formed flint blades with razor-sharp edges. Some of these are broken to form microliths which, for example, can be fixed to straight twigs to form barbed arrows or harpoons. One of the best-known sites of this period, and the one which, by using the Carbon 14 technique, has provided the earliest date for the culture in Britain, is known as Thatcham. In fact several sites of temporary camps were discovered on a terrace of higher ground near the Kennet to the south-east of the sewage works in Lower Way. The site was originally recognised in 1921 by Harold Peake and O.G.S. Crawford but it was from excavations led by John Wymer from 1958–61 that material was recovered which produced the Carbon 14 date of about 10,000 years ago. In 1989/90 the Trust for Wessex Archaeology carried out further excavations nearby on behalf of Thames Water.

During this period the watery area of the Kennet Valley was more extensive than at present. Modern archaeologists consider that the river was 'braided', that is divided into many streams. On the other hand Harold Peake was convinced that there were several lakes in the valley, dams being formed by beavers whose bones he had found. Whichever is correct it seems likely that fish in the river or lakes were a source of food as were waterfowl which were probably particularly plentiful in the autumn and winter. The valley seems also to have provided a major routeway from the Thames and Rhine in the east to western Britain. Many sites have been discovered between Thatcham and Hungerford, largely by Roy Froom, which date from throughout the six thousand years which the Middle Stone Age lasted. Evidence of a major site in the Lambourn Valley was discovered at Bagnor, during the construction of the Newbury by-pass.

An artist's impression of the Mesolithic site on the River Kennet near Thatcham. (Artist Liz James. Reproduced by kind permission of Thames Water and the Trust for Wessex Archaeology)

The final period of the Stone Age, which archaeologists call the Neolithic or New Stone Age, marks one of the greatest stages in man's development. From around 6,300 years ago groups of people came to Britain from mainland Europe bringing with them a completely new set of skills. These important new skills related to farming. For the first time man began to have control of his food supply and could cease the nomadic way of life which all his ancestors had followed. These first farmers had learnt to grow primitive forms of wheat and barley and also kept domesticated strains of cattle, sheep or goat and pig.

Apart from the animals he kept and the grain and other plants which he grew 'man the farmer' and his way of life had other effects on the environment. He would need to clear areas of forest to provide space to grow his crops and to build enclosures or stockades in which to keep his animals. The forest may partly have been cleared by burning but a great number of trees must have been cut down with stone axes. Several complete stone axe heads and parts of many broken ones have been found in the Newbury area.

Being settled in one place allowed man to build a more substantial and comfortable home and presumably he would begin to accumulate more possessions than would have been practical for a nomad. It also seems likely that people would feel that an area of land around their homes was their property. In other words it is in the Neolithic period that we see the beginnings of modern society.

Although many flint implements from this period have been found in the Newbury area no settlement site has been positively identified. A saddle quern – a stone on which corn was ground – was found at Newtown Common and fragments of pottery have been discovered in several areas. The most obvious proof of habitation by Neolithic people is long barrows. These are the earthen mounds in which remains of the dead were interred. Sometimes they contained chambers formed from gigantic stones of which 'Wayland's Smithy' (on the Ridgeway north of Lambourn) is our nearest example. It is at the eastern edge of the area in which such barrows are found. There is a long barrow amongst many later round barrows at Lambourn Seven Barrows and another near Inkpen on which Combe Gibbet is erected. The ditches which flanked the sides of the barrow, from which the earth was dug to create it, can also be seen. The ditches have become almost refilled with the passage of time and similarly the barrow, which would at first have gleamed white from the freshly dug chalk, now merges with the grass covered hilltop.

Probably a little less than 4,500 years ago there began a significant incursion of people with new ideas from mainland Europe. This new era is called the Bronze Age. Not surprisingly they had cultural practices which differed from those of the Neolithic people. Most notably they buried the remains of their dead leaders singly, beneath a circular mound surrounded by a ditch. From excavated examples it has been found that subsidiary burials may have been made in the edges of the mounds. Three good examples of these mounds, known as round barrows, can be seen at the recreation ground at Wash Common, although the ditches have filled with soil over the centuries. There is also a disc barrow and it is likely that many further burials took place in the spaces between the barrows. The whole area of this Bronze Age cemetery is included in the list of ancient monuments of national importance.

The earliest people to cross from the Continent are sometimes known as 'Beaker Folk' from the name given to a distinctive type of decorated pottery vessel which they used. In West Berkshire Museum there is an undamaged beaker which is the finest example in the country of a type whose decoration shows it to be linked with people from the Middle Rhine area of what is now Germany. This vessel was found at Inkpen with a four-footed bowl with the same cultural origins. Fragments of other beakers have been found in the area as have very large pottery vessels in which cremated remains were sometimes buried.

Bronze was first used to make axes as land clearance for farming was still of great importance. The design of axe heads, and the casting technology needed, developed very quickly. Soon a whole range of implements, swords, spearheads, knives, gouges and awls as well as decorative items were being made. Alongside these metal tools finely-made stone hammers and delicate but efficient flint arrowheads were in use. There is considerable evidence of Bronze Age activity in the whole of the Newbury area, both valley and downland. Field boundaries, ploughed-down barrows and other monuments can be identified from aerial photography but few habitation sites have been found in the immediate area. Preliminary excavation in advance of building development and gravel extraction to the north and east of Thatcham identified possible habitation sites. During the development of Conifer Crest at Wash Common two baked clay weights from a weaving loom were discovered which could indicate a building in that area. During archaeological investigations connected with the construction of the Newbury by-pass, a few features and pottery fragments of Bronze Age date were found at a number of locations towards the northern end of the route, suggesting habitation of that period. Also, an extensive and substantial scatter of worked flint of late Neolithic or Bronze Age date (c 3000–1500 BC) was investigated. This ran north from the Fox and Hounds pub, along the dry valley in which the former A34 ran. Whilst these indicated human activity from those eras, any clear evidence of settlement seems to have been destroyed by ploughing over many centuries. About 20 metres south of the flint scatter, a complete Middle-Bronze Age (c 1500–1100 BC) urn was found, but again no other clear evidence of occupation.

The Bronze Age culture continued until around 2,500 years ago but about two centuries before it came to an end the influence of another Continental culture becomes apparent. At one time it was believed that there had been invasions from Europe. In recent years archaeologists have come to believe that the new technologies were adopted by Britons following ideas and designs learnt through their extensive trading with the European mainland. Some people from the mainland may well have settled in Britain but there is no evidence of large scale movement.

But there were significant developments in the organisation of society and the materials used. A new name is attached to the people once the new systems became widespread. They are known variously as Iron Age people, Celts or Ancient Britons, for these are the people whom the Romans conquered after their invasion of 43 AD. They became skilled in iron as well as bronze and also used gold, silver and other metals.

Iron Age people seem to have had a highly organised society. The country was divided up into large tribal areas. For example the Attrebate tribe had a regional 'capital' at Silchester (which the Romans called Calleva Atrebatum). They also built many hill forts, defensible positions surrounded by high banks and ditches and with complex entrances. It should be noted that some hill forts had been built during the Bronze Age. Some forts may have been occupied almost permanently whilst others

A group of three iron age gold coins discovered near Hampstead Norreys. (West Berkshire Museum)

were resorted to at times of danger. They were intended to hold herds of animals as well as people. There are fifteen hill forts within a few miles of Newbury. Beacon Hill near Highclere and Walbury Hill near Inkpen, which enclosed an extremely large area, are the most accessible.

The famous White Horse cut into the hillside at Uffington is believed to date from this period. It could either be tribal insignia or the symbol of a god. Horses appear on many of the gold or silver coins which were in use after 100 BC and the design of many of these is similar to the Uffington Horse.

Objects from the Iron Age are comparatively rare. This is partly due to the short duration of this period when compared with earlier ones. Pottery fragments and indications of occupation have been found in the Newbury-Thatcham area and also in the Aldermaston and Beenham areas, where sites were excavated in advance of gravel extraction from the 1970s onwards. Grain storage pits and other features have been found at Beedon. A number of metal objects have been recovered by users of metal detectors. These include silver coins in the downland area north of Newbury and near Kintbury, whilst one gold coin was found at Wash

Common and three, struck from the same die, were found in 1979 near Hampstead Norreys. A decorative ring through which the reins of a chariot passed was discovered nearby. A fine early Iron Age bronze brooch was recovered at Northcroft and a decorative bronze pin and brooch fragments have been found in the Lambourn Valley.

Although Julius Caesar sent expeditionary forces to Britain in 55 and 54 BC the Roman conquest of Britain was only attempted and achieved following the invasion during the reign of the Emperor Claudius in 43 AD. The power of the Roman army was, of course, eventually successful in defeating the British tribes, but it is not true that they drove all Britons into Wales and the west. For most farmworkers or craftsmen it probably made little difference whether they were under the control of an Iron Age chieftain or a Roman. For example, although the shapes of Roman pottery were standardised throughout their empire Iron Age influences continued to be shown in pottery in early Roman Britain.

The first network of Roman roads was built for military purposes, but during the four centuries of Roman rule there is evidence that this network was modified. There may also have been minor roads which did not need to be built to the high standards of the major routeways and have thus left no identified trace. Silchester was an important Roman town and the walls which surrounded it are still intact. One of the major Roman roads radiating from Silchester crosses the River Kennet near Colthrop, east of Thatcham, probably passed through Shaw and then, near Wickham, divided. The northern branch continued to Gloucester whilst the other went to Bath. Two Roman route descriptions relating to these roads survive from the second century, both list a settlement 'Spinae'. From its name present-day Speen would appear to be the successor to the Roman settlement but so far there is insufficient archaeological evidence to support this. It would seem more likely that the site is yet to be discovered in an undeveloped area.

Romans were present in the area of Newbury as shown by pottery found in several places, some of which dates from the period of the conquest. A cemetery was discovered in 1856 when the railway goods yard was being made. This site is immediately east of the present A339, at the rear of the Sainsbury's site. Unfortunately little was recorded of the discovery except that there were at least one hundred burials, some being

Pottery including Samian Ware bowls recovered from the Roman cemetery in Newbury. (West Berkshire Museum)

cremations indicating that the cemetery was in use over a long period. The settlement it served could thus have been quite small. Three sites to the west of Newbury were located during the construction of the by-pass. These were an early first century site between Enborne Road and the railway; this site was also occupied in the late third and fourth centuries. Roman features were also found at Elmore Plantation, Speen and a farmstead site was discovered near Bagnor. The latter also had finds indicating use both early in the Roman period and in the third/fourth centuries. The well-preserved underground structure of a corn dryer was recorded; this appeared to have fallen out of use in the fourth century. Parts of a small village occupied in the third and fourth centuries were excavated at the western edge of Thatcham in the late 1920s, more or less on the line of the present A4 road. And of course there is evidence of an extensive Roman villa complex at Littlecote where excavations revealed the famous mosaic.

Britain was important to the Roman Empire because of its mineral resources and suitability for farming, especially grain growing and sheep rearing. Evidence from the downland north of Newbury indicates intensive farming activities. Pottery making was carried out at Aldworth, Shaw and Hamstead Marshall in the third and fourth centuries. Pottery fragments, coins and other objects have been found throughout the area and are too numerous to detail here.

The Romans officially withdrew from Britain in AD 410, though leaving behind many people of Roman, or part Roman, origin. For over a century they had had to contend with raids along the coasts by Saxons and others from northern Europe. With the army gone these raiders eventually conquered much of Britain. However, there is no historical record of these events and the archaeological record is also sparse. Much of what was recorded later is based on folklore and myth. It is not until the invaders were converted to Christianity after the arrival of a number of missionaries in the 7th century that literate monks begin again to record our history.

Several place names in the area have Saxon origins and when records of the boundaries of manors begin to survive from around the late 9th century then it becomes clear that most of our villages and towns were established in Saxon times. The 'Domesday Book' of 1086 further confirms this. This book recorded who held what land of the King and what it was worth at the time of the Norman Conquest of 1066 as well as in the year when it was written.

Although there was a Saxon settlement called Ulvritone somewhere close to Newbury, the town as such was not begun until after the Norman Conquest. This is made clear in the Domesday Book as the value of Ulvritone is shown to be greatly increased by 1086 and also there are 51 'hagae' or plots of town land.

William the Conqueror had let most of the land of Britain to Norman lords in return for services given and promised for the future. Several of these lords, wishing to increase the value of their land, gained the permission of the King to develop new towns. In return the King would have required payment or for the lord to provide him with additional goods or services, such as a number of armed men to help fight his battles.

Ernulf de Hesdin was one such lord and the 51 plots referred to in Domesday are plots in his new town – 'Newbury'. Ernulf de Hesdin held 47 manors in addition to that of Newbury. Unfortunately for him, he was falsely accused before William II and, although he proved his innocence by combat, he relinquished his lands and journeyed to the Holy Land in 1096. He died at Antioch. The Newbury plots were available for craftsmen and traders to rent and on which they would build their houses and workshops. The archaeological excavations in Bartholomew Street in 1979 and Cheap Street in 1981 confirmed this development. There were no Saxon buildings on either site and in fact evidence of Saxon ploughing was found in Bartholomew Street. Also on that site was substantial evidence of two buildings of around the year 1100, which must have been amongst the original buildings of Newbury. It is interesting that the southern boundary of these structures continued to be used by successive buildings up until those that were demolished in 1978.

During excavations of the Cheap Street site it was found that the land had been lower-lying and more marshy than Bartholomew Street and that the erection of buildings had commenced some decades later. The bed of a ditch or stream running along the line of the frontage of the buildings, and which had been first found in excavations of 1973/74, was also discovered. This may have contributed to the dampness of the Cheap Street site but could also have provided the power to drive a watermill. A worn stone bearing, probably from an early watermill, was found in 1876 when the Town Hall was being built nearby.

It has long been thought that there was a castle somewhere in the centre of Newbury and it is possible that it was an original feature of the planned town. However, the only record of it which has been traced relates to it being besieged in 1152/3. The castle was held for Matilda by John Marshal who had to hand over his son, William, as a hostage. It was captured by Stephen after a siege of over 2 months. According to a poem written about 60 years after the event Stephen threatened William with many forms of death, but the boy grew up to become the Earl of Pembroke and the Great Protector. References to the castle existing at later dates, quoted by Walter Money and others, have been shown to be erroneous through research in 1990 by Paul Cannon of West Berkshire Museum. Additionally, investigations at Hamstead Marshall, where there are three castle mounds and a medieval village site, lead me to think it possible that the so-called Siege of Newbury may actually have been at Hamstead Marshall. Newbury was amongst the largest towns in the country at this period. It is feasible that a village three miles to its west could be referred to by the name of its better-known neighbour.

CHAPTER TWO

The Middle Ages and the Descent of the Manor

After the departure of Ernulf de Hesdin, as referred to in the previous chapter, his forty eight manors were divided into three parts. Those manors in Berkshire came into the possession of the Chaworth (or Cadurcis) family, and the Counts of Perche. Whether they were held by them as heirs of Ernulf of whether they were a regrant of the confiscated lands by William II is uncertain.

In 1166 Newbury was in the hands of Payne de Montdublel of the Chaworth family. He held it until 1189 when it returned to the Crown. It passed to the Counts of Perche. Geoffrey, the 4th count, and his wife, Matilda, founded Sandleford Priory, but he died in France in 1202 when he was on his way to take part in a Crusade.

When King Philip of France confiscated the Normandy possessions of King John he promptly retaliated by seizing the manors of the Normans in England. The King dispossessed the Countess of Perche and her son, Thomas, of the manor of Newbury in 1204.

King John was intimately connected with Newbury. His favourite hunting seat was at Freemantle Park, Kingsclere. He came to the town in 1200 accompanied by his natural son Geoffrey. According to legend, John was hidden in a cottage of an old Newbury spinning woman when he fled from the insurgent barons, one reason suggested for his foundation of St Bartholomew's Hospital, and the grant of a fair for its maintenance.

In 1204 John granted the manor to Robert Fitz-Roger, but no further information is known of his ownership. Fawkes de Breaute and John's son, Geoffrey Fitzroy, both received revenues and land in the manor. Eventually it appears that John regranted Newbury to Thomas, Earl of Perche and Marshal of France, but Thomas fell at the Battle of Lincoln on 19th May 1217, where he led the French forces against the army of the young King Henry III, which were under the command of William Marshal, Earl of Pembroke. His lands were forfeited and once again Newbury returned to the Crown. It was granted by Henry III to his uncle, William Longspé, Earl of Salisbury, the illegitimate son of Henry II by the Fair Rosamund Clifford.

However, the nephew and heir of the Count of Perche, William, Bishop of Chalon-sur-Marne, came to England to claim his uncle's estates. The claim was evidently recognised for the Bishop sold Newbury to William Marshal, 2nd Earl of Pembroke, who had succeeded to the earldom on the death of his father in 1219. The first Earl, of course, had been the boy threatened by King Stephen during the Siege of Newbury. The manor was confirmed to the second Earl in 1220.

The descent of the manor was destined to become complicated. The 2nd Earl died without issue, and his estates passed in turn to his four brothers, all of whom died childless so that the vast possessions of the Marshals then passed to the five sisters of the family and their heirs.

At first, Newbury was held by Eleanor, the widow of the second earl and sister of Henry III. She held it as part of her dower, and brought it to her second husband, Simon de Montfort, whom she married in 1238.

Upon de Montfort's death at the Battle of Evesham in 1265, Newbury was claimed by Gilbert, Earl of Gloucester but was taken into the hands of the Crown by King Edward I in 1274 while the division of the Marshal estates continued.

In the following year the borough sent two members to Parliament, and Newbury had become one of the great English centres of craftsmen. After 1316 the Mortimer branch of the Marshal family became the chief holders of land and manorial rights in Newbury; but in that year the town is not mentioned among the Berkshire boroughs. However, in 1377 with a population calculated as 1,900, Newbury was larger than Reading and the 37th largest town in the country. There was a population increase to 2,690 by 1525; despite this the town had been overtaken by Reading but still retained a similar position in the ranking of towns by their population. In terms of taxable wealth Newbury was the 20th and 21st wealthiest town in 1377 and 1525 respectively. But it was in the later 16th and 17th centuries that both Newbury and its neighbour declined because of the fall in demand for their main product – broadcloth. In the early 15th century Newbury was held by Edmund Mortimer, Earl of March. He died without issue in 1425, and Newbury passed to his sister's son, Richard, Duke of York.

The Borough of Newbury

Having the status of a borough was important to a town. Essentially, boroughs were governed in a quite different way from the surrounding countryside and the inhabitants had much greater freedom in deciding their affairs. Essentially they were manufacturing and trading centres. Usually they were self-governed by a mayor and corporation elected by the burgesses; the leading craftsmen and merchants of the town. In the Middle Ages goods were not sold in shops or from workplaces, but only in markets. The right to hold a market was thus an important privilege. Some form of payment would be made to the monarch for the right to hold a market and in turn those granted the market would be able to charge a toll or fee on everything sold. A successful market would enable craftsmen, or country folk bringing in their surplus products for sale, to receive a better price than selling to their immediate community. A good market could bring in people from a wide area. Fairs were another important privilege.

Newbury's name, literally, is 'new borough', in effect meaning 'new market town'. Although the evidence is only circumstantial, it appears likely that the status of borough was granted to Ernulf de Hesdin as lord of the manor of Ulvritone/Newbury. Thus it became a profitable activity of the manor, rather than being fully independent. The borough would be under the control of the lord of the manor of Newbury, which for much of its earlier history was the monarch. It is only with the grant of a charter to the town by Queen Elizabeth in 1596 that the Borough of Newbury becomes a truly independent town. A few years later, in 1627, the Borough purchased a grant of the manor from King Charles I, thus completely reversing the way in which the town was originally governed.

The Wars of the Roses

The Duke of York's ownership of the manor involved Newbury in the Wars of the Roses, and the town was taken by the Earl of Wiltshire in 1460, when many of the inhabitants were executed as traitors for supporting the White Rose, and the other townsmen were deprived of all their possessions. Richard fell at Wakefield in the same year, and his son became King Edward IV in the following year when Newbury was regarded as a royal appanage. The King granted the manor and borough to his mother, Cecily, Duchess of York.

The Grant of Fairs

In the fifth year of his reign King Edward IV gave a grant of two fairs to Newbury, each to last four days. The first was to be held on the eve of the feast of Corpus Christi, on the day of the same feast, and for two days following, and the second on the eve of the Nativity of St John the Baptist, on the day of the same feast, and for two days following. The Crown reserved to itself two thirds of the profits of the two fairs, the other third was granted to the King's 'trusty and beloved servant, Thomas Herbert, the elder, and his heirs male, in consideration of the good, gratuitous, and laudable service'. The granting of fairs in this way was a very commonly used method of raising revenue by the Crown during the Middle Ages.

The Duke of Buckingham's Insurrection

On 18th October 1483, the town was one of the meeting places for those who supported the Duke of Buckingham's rising when it was hoped to overthrow Richard III in favour of Henry Tudor, Earl of Richmond. The plot failed. Buckingham was beheaded at Salisbury. Two years later Richard was killed at Bosworth Field, the Tudor dynasty was established and Newbury was in the hands of Henry VII.

Henry VIII granted Newbury first to Anne Boleyn and then to Jane Seymour. Edward VI granted it to his sister Princess Elizabeth, later Queen, who made her first visit to the town in 1568.

Borough Charters

Elizabeth granted the earliest existing charter to the Borough in 1596. (References to Burgesses in 1189 and Town Bailiffs in 1204 indicate that there was some sort of independent town government well before the 1596 Charter.) It ordained government of the town by a council consisting of 31 burgesses, which included the Mayor and six aldermen. There were to be five companies for the principal trades. Tanners: including barbers and surgeons; Mercers: including all provision dealers and apothecaries; Clothiers (Tailors): including scriveners and schoolmasters; Weavers or clothmakers; Braziers: including builders.

Four fairs were also appointed, to be held annually, one on the day of the Annunciation (25th March), one on St John the Baptist's day (24th June), one on St Bartholomew's day (24th August) and the last on St Simon and St Jude's day (28th October).

Revocations and renewals of the charter were made by Charles I, Charles II and James II.

James I granted the manor of Newbury to his Queen, Anne of Denmark, and together they visited the town in 1603, the year before an outbreak of the plague struck the town causing the deaths of many inhabitants. The last grant took place in 1627 when, on payment of a quit rent, Charles I granted the manor to the Mayor and Corporation of Newbury.

Greenham Preceptory of Knights Hospitallers

There are no visible remains of the preceptory which, at one time, was believed to have stood near the site of the present Police Station in Mill Lane. This belief had come about due to confusion over the origins of stone-built walls and buildings on Newbury and Greenham wharves. Some historians have thought that the Stone Building at The Wharf was a remaining section of Newbury Castle and that the nearby walls of the same sort of stone were a re-use of the castle's building material for the preceptory. We now know that the building was an early 19th century construction of the Kennet and Avon Canal Company, using stone from its quarries near Bath. The walls around the adjoining Greenham Wharf demarcated the property which the Company had purchased, from that of Newbury Wharf which it leased from Kendrick's Charity. A fragment of the wall survives behind the Police Station.

Wherever the preceptory was, and a site nearer to Greenham church seems more likely, it was an interesting institution of the Middle Ages. Established in the reign of Henry VII, the inmates in 1338 were the Preceptor, a brother knight, a chaplain, a squire, a bailiff, with several under officers and servants. Another house of this order at Shalford, near Brimpton, was run in conjunction with Greenham. The order was suppressed by Henry VIII in 1540, but Greenham was revived for a short time in the reign of Mary, to be finally suppressed when Elizabeth ascended the throne.

Sandleford Priory

The Priory of St John the Baptist at Sandleford was founded between 1193 and 1200 by Geoffrey, Count of Perche and lord of Newbury, for Augustinian canons. It was one of the smaller priories with never more than six canons and only three in 1274. A project for increasing the endowments and turning the house into a great Benedictine convent of the order of Fontevrault for 40 nuns and 10 chaplains never materialised. Edward II stayed here in 1320, and a royal pensioner was lodged in the priory. Prior Simon Dam was deposed in 1440 being accused of allowing the house to become ruinous, and of other faults. The priory never recovered and being left vacant by the death of the last canon in 1478, the estates and buildings were granted to St George's Chapel, Windsor. The church remained functioning under a stipendiary priest until about 1534. In 1614 it was recorded that the building was in a decayed state and unfit for the holding of services.

The priory was converted into a dwelling house and experienced a number of lessees for almost 200 years until 1668 when it came into the hands of the Kingsmill family who restored it as a private dwelling. In 1730 it passed into the hands of Edward Montagu, a grandson of the Earl of Sandwich. Edward married the beautiful and clever Elizabeth Robinson who acquired fame as the reputed founder of the Blue Stocking Club. Some of the most brilliant men of the day were entertained at Sandleford.

On being left a widow in 1775 Elizabeth Montagu devoted her energies to the improvement of the property. James Wyatt was her architect and Lancelot (Capability) Brown supervised the laying out of the extensive gardens. Externally, especially the elevation seen from the road, the priory remains much as it appeared following Wyatt's work. He extended the house and remodelled it in the Gothic style between 1780 and 1786.

In 1835 the priory was leased by Mr William Chatteris, who also improved the property. He had a particular interest in gardens and over a period of years planted near to the lakes what was then the finest

Hospital of St Bartholomew, Argyle Road. (Author)

collection of azaleas and rhododendrons in England. He purchased the freehold of the property from the Dean and Chapter of Windsor in 1871 to ensure his future at the priory. The large mansion, now St Gabriel's School, incorporates some of the old monastic walls, notably of the choir and priory church with its interesting timber roof. Of the later renovations, Mrs Montagu's charming oval drawing room is used once again for musical and dramatic presentations when the present occupants entertain their guests.

Hospital of St Bartholomew

It is believed that King John founded the Hospital of St Bartholomew in Newbury, but the charter is lost; however, he granted the fair of two days in 1215 which was held annually until the last war. The hospital was for a priest warden, who is sometimes called prior, with brethren and sisters living under religious vows and caring for the aged and sick. It was not suppressed at the Reformation, and became almshouses, the present interesting range dating from 1618 – see page 183.

The Litten Chapel, built c1480, from an oil painting of around 1835. The picture looks southward down Newtown Road, with Argyle Road forking to the right. (West Berkshire Museum)

Litten Chapel

To the north is the 15th century chapel of the hospital, called the Litten Chapel. It is attached to the old Grammar School of 1849 (now offices) at the junction of Pound Street and Newtown Road. The east end of the chapel is often reported to have been shortened in 1825 when Newtown Road was widened. But the alteration must have been before that date, as a plan of the area drawn before 1814 and a print of the chapel stating that it was cut 'prior to its alteration in 1826' both show the chapel as its current length. In the north wall were formerly two square-headed windows, each of two lights, of the decorated period; but one of these has been converted into a doorway. There is a window of a later date in the south wall with a modern doorway.

The gabled roof with its carved and moulded queen posts dates from 1480 although the tie beams have been removed. The moulded purlins have curved wind braces and many timbers are profusely carved with Tudor roses. The chapel has now been converted into offices.

St Mary's

Another hospital, dedicated to St Mary Magdalen for leprous women, is recorded in 1232. It is possible that the name was changed to The House of Blessed Mary, a hospital of sisters which appears in a deed of 1375. No further records have been found and the house may have become St Mary's Almshouses for six poor women which was in existence, near the southern end of Cheap Street, in 1604, and was then considered ancient. These almshouses were in use until 1967.

Donnington Friary

A Chapel of Jesus was rebuilt at Donnington by Sir Richard Abberbury after 1365, and in 1376 he granted the endowments to the Priory of the Crouched Friars in London, on condition that two friars should live there and serve the chapel. A Priory of the Crouched Friars was established, and a conventual chapel was built on the north side of the

Jesus Chapel which was taken from the friars in 1448 as they had not fulfilled the conditions. The priory was suppressed in 1538, being surrendered by two friars who claimed to be the Trinitarian Order, but this was probably a ruse through which they hoped to gain pensions. The Jesus Chapel was suppressed as a chantry in 1546. A large house called The Priory occupies the site and now serves as offices and showrooms for Dreweatt-Neate, the old established fine art auctioneers.

Donnington Hospital

The picturesque Donnington Hospital stands between the bridges over the River Lambourn on the west side of Oxford Road. It was founded in 1393 by Sir Richard Abberbury who endowed it with revenues from his manor of Iffley in Oxfordshire. It was built for thirteen poor men, one of whom was to act as master with the title of God's Minister. The inmates attended services in the chapel of the friary to pray for the welfare of the founder and his family, and then for the souls of the departed.

One of the almsmen, Thomas Barrie, was accused in 1538 of spreading a rumour that Henry VIII was dead, and he was made to stand all day in Newbury Market Place with his ears nailed to the pillory. At the end of the day both his ears were cut off. A cruel fate for an old man.

At the Reformation the hospital was not suppressed, but the revenues were confiscated by the Crown. Queen Elizabeth restored the revenues in 1570, and with the Earl of Nottingham she refounded the almshouses as 'The Hospital of Queen Elizabeth', in 1602.

The buildings suffered considerable damage during the period of the Civil War and the inmates were housed elsewhere. In spite of the heirs of the Earl of Nottingham retaining the title of Patron it fell to the lot of the then lord of the manor, Robert Packer, to restore the almshouses after the war. He was assisted by his younger brother, William, who had the satisfaction of seeing the almsmen rehoused in the renovated hospital before he died in 1679. In 1681 the 3rd Earl of Nottingham died without issue and the patronage passed to the Packer family.

A descendant, the Reverend Winchcombe Hartley, lord of the manors of Bucklebury and Donnington, extensively renovated the almshouses in 1822. Late in the 20th century internal alterations provided modern amenities for the residents.

Above the doorway are the gilded arms of Queen Elizabeth I and inside the porch are the old weathered stone arms which were originally on the front.

This charity, founded so many centuries ago, continues to flourish with additional homes in Abberbury Close, Donnington, Bucklebury and Iffley.

Donnington Castle

Sir Richard Abberbury also altered Donnington Castle (built around fifty years earlier) after he had received the necessary royal licence in 1386. A substantial change which he made was the building of a strong new entrance with a portcullis and guarded by two cylindrical towers. This comprises the major part of the remains which survive today. Edward VI stayed here in 1552, and Queen Elizabeth granted the castle to the Earl of Nottingham, Baron Howard of Effingham, in 1600, as a reward for services against the Spanish Armada. The story of the gallant defence of the castle by Colonel Sir John Boys during the Civil War will be found later under the Battles of Newbury. The great Gate House remains to almost its full height and is a fine example of 14th century military architecture. It is built of flint with stone dressings and consists of three main storeys with tall circular flanking towers on each side of the main gateway. The archway of the gate is four-centred with a label. The string-courses are ornamental with grotesque heads. The walls have been pitted in a number of places by the cannonballs fired during the sieges and brick patching has been necessary in places. A cottage which was built on to the back in the 19th century has been demolished. The entrance way on the ground floor has lovely and intricate stone vaulting springing from attached shafts. A newel stair in the southern flanking tower leads to the upper floors. The first floor has a large square-headed window retaining some of its tracery. A number of important buildings were formerly attached to the west side of the Gate House which probably included the great hall on the first floor, and in the wall are several doorways, fireplaces and windows. The foundations of the curtain walls can be traced to the west, and the castle was originally some

Donnington Castle – the Gate House.

150 feet (45.7m) long and 93 feet (28.4m) wide. The monument is in the care of English Heritage.

Winchester College Hostelry

A hostelry was established in Newbury in the mid-15th century by Winchester College for students and travellers between Winchester and New College, Oxford. It stood in Northcroft Lane facing Pembroke Road and was a long medieval building of two storeys. Parts of this building were considered to date from the 13th century and to have been relics of a still earlier hostelry possibly established by King John but first recorded in 1223 as belonging to Henry III. The whole building was pulled down in 1934 (*Transactions of Newbury Field Club*, vol vii, p3).

Grammar School

There is some controversy about the date of the founding of Newbury Grammar School. For many years it has been stated that Henry Wormestall founded it in 1466 as part of his chantry foundation, but research by Norman Fox has contradicted this belief. The Wormestall claim was based on a reading of documents related to the suppression of chantry chapels between 1546 and 1548 and interpreting these as meaning that a school was part of the original foundation of the chantry.

There were two chantries connected with St Nicolas' church – Wormestall's and Warmington's. In the responses of the churchwardens and priest to enquiries by the Chantry Commissioners in 1546, there is no provision for a schoolmaster or school recorded for either of them. This is likely to be an accurate representation of the position, as they would have had a vested interest in holding on to a school, should one have existed. But, when they make their responses to questions arising from the 1547 act, a major part of the incomes of both chantries are shown as supporting schoolmasters teaching at the grammar school. These masters were also the priests of each chantry and so it appears that their duties had been modified.

It therefore seems likely that between 1546 and 1548 the trustees of the chantries had decided to alter the terms of the chantry foundations, as they were entitled to do. Perhaps this was to ensure that the income of the chantry foundations continued to be of benefit to the town and were not confiscated by the King. At the same time it was also decided to convert the chapel of St Bartholomew's Hospital to a schoolhouse – 'of which the town had great need'. The Chantry Commissioners found that the Warmington's priest was too old and awarded him a pension, but continued the payment to the former Wormestall's Chantry priest as a schoolmaster. This therefore seems to be the origin of Newbury Grammar School.

Larger premises were provided in 1849 by rebuilding the residence next to the former St Bartholomew's Hospital chapel (also known as the Litten Chapel). In 1885 it was transferred to a new school with spacious playing fields in Enborne Road. Then, in September 1975, it was merged with the former County Girls' Grammar School (founded 1909) in Andover Road to form the present establishment.

Medieval Roads

Perhaps a significant reason for the continuity of Newbury's market, when others in the area eventually failed, and for the town's relative prosperity, was its position in the medieval road network. Several roads met at Newbury where, for centuries, there had been a way to cross the wide and marshy valley of the River Kennet. From at least the Middle Ages the north-south road had been important, running from the port of Southampton and the ecclesiastical centre of Winchester to Oxford and the Midlands. Oxford had been a seat of learning from the mid-13th century and, as mentioned above, in the 15th century Winchester College had built (or modified an existing building) a hostel in Newbury for use by students travelling between the two places. The influential Bishop of Winchester, William of Wykeham, had founded New College, Oxford in 1379 and Winchester College in 1382. It is also of interest to note that 15th century records of the port of Southampton show large quantities of wine being transported to Oxford. This too must have passed through Newbury.

As it entered Newbury, the road used the present Old Newtown Road and Derby Road into the settlement around St Bartholomew's Hospital – later known as 'The City'. The road from Salisbury via Andover to Oxford diverted from its present line north of Buckingham Road to cross what is now the City Recreation Ground into Hampton Road where it joined the Winchester road to form the present Argyle Road and then northwards along Bartholomew Street. The road to and from Basingstoke seems also to have provided a route to Chichester and the medieval port of Shoreham, near Brighton. This port would have been important to England's wool and cloth merchants. Until 1950, when it was diverted to run from the Swan Inn at Newtown, the road crossed Greenham Common, from the present route of the A339 at Knight's Bridge (north-west of Headley), to the southern end of Greenham Road. It then passed down Pyle Hill and Cheap Street to the Market Place where it turned sharply west to join the Winchester and Salisbury roads.

North of the town the Oxford road divided just north of Donnington, to provided a route to Wantage and the Cotswold Hills, the latter being an important source of wool. The main east-west road ran along the northern flank of the Kennet Valley, passing through Speenhamland (around the Broadway) where it was joined by the roads from the south. Seven hundred yards to the east of this junction a road, now Shaw Road and Long Lane, took travellers north-east to the crossing of the Thames from Streatley to Goring and then along the Chiltern Hills and onwards to East Anglia. Today this seems a minor road, but it has as its origin one of the oldest routes in the country as the Thames crossing has been important since pre-historic times. The routeways from the south could also have formed a link with the Streatley route from the pre-historic ridgeway along the Hampshire downs, as some think that Northbrook Street represents an ancient raised causeway across the Kennet Valley.

CHAPTER THREE

The Late Middle Ages and the Cloth Trade

The prosperity and trade of Newbury grew in the 15th century when the town became world-famous for its weaving. The principal business centres were the Market Place, which had stallages and shambles, and the northern sections of Cheap Street and Bartholomew Street.

Jack of Newbury

Towards the end of the 15th century, the cloth trade produced Newbury's greatest hero, John Smallwood, also known as John Winchcombe – after the place in Gloucestershire where he is thought to have been born. As he achieved fame he became known as 'Jack of Newbury'.

There is difficulty in separating fact from myth in the story of his achievements, which is further complicated by his son having the same names and succeeding to his father's business. The popular version of the story is that when he had reached the age of fifteen, his parents sent him to the great abbey at Winchcombe, with the intention that he should become a monk. But before he had taken any vows he felt that he was not at all suited to a celibate monastic life and so he ran away. Coming to Newbury, he was apprenticed to a rich cloth-maker, and when his master died he married Alice, the wealthy young widow. It appears that the two had been indulging in a mild flirtation during the master's lifetime, and after Alice

Jack of Newbury – from the brass in St Nicolas' church.

became a widow, she chose Jack, though there were many more prosperous suitors; and the wedding took place in the Litten Chapel. It was not a very happy match as Alice was lively and frivolous, and there is a story that one night when she came home very late, Jack refused to let her in. At last he relented to her entreaties; but when he had let her in she pretended that she had dropped her ring outside. When Jack kindly went out to look for it she slammed the door and locked it, keeping him outside in his night-shirt for the remainder of the night. Before long Alice died, leaving all her wealth and the flourishing business to Jack. But he soon married again, this time Joan, the daughter of a poor man from Aylesbury; but a most sumptuous wedding took place. Jack extended the cloth-making business to such a degree that he may be said to have erected the first true factory in England, with 200 looms and employing nearly 1,000 men, women and children. The factory stretched from his house in Northbrook Street to the Marsh, now Victoria Park. Jack was ordered to provide four pikemen and two horsemen for the King's army during the war with Scotland. But he gathered and equipped a force of 50 pikemen and 50 horsemen, leading them in person. A contemporary poem tells how the lads of Newbury distinguished themselves at the Battle of Flodden in 1513, though some writers have maintained that the Newbury force was not in time for the battle. Jack entertained Henry VIII and his first queen, Catherine of Aragon (1516–18), when the king wished to dub him knight, but Jack begged to be excused the honour as he preferred to remain a plain man among his work people. Jack died soon afterwards in 1519, and was succeeded by his son, also John Winchcombe, to whom, in 1540, Henry VIII sold the confiscated Reading Abbey estates at Bucklebury and Thatcham for a payment of £2,419 13s 4d. A portrait of the second John Winchcombe can be seen in the Museum.

Jack of Newbury's House

Jack of Newbury's house in Northbrook Street once extended southwards from Marsh Lane to include the present Marks & Spencer's shop and possibly further. All that now remains is a small northern section and its decorated gable end can be seen in Marsh Lane. It can be seen that the building is of timber-framed construction, the spaces between the timbers being filled with brick, some in a herring-bone pattern. The first

Jack of Newbury's house, now 24 Northbrook Street; picture taken c1913.

floor overhangs the street and has delicate carved brackets, moulded and carved ornamentation of the woodwork and a delightful oriel window. The gable again overhangs this and has one surviving decorated bargeboard. The private upper floors have original timber work too and the roof timbers and chimney stack also appear to be part of the late 15th century building.

During demolition of buildings to the south (where Tesco Metro now stands) at the beginning of the 20th century, curious carved panels were recorded and photographed. On one of the panels was a raised bust, believed to be of John Winchcombe, accompanied by the initials I.W. On either side his two wives, Alice and Joan, were represented. Another carving represented the Trinity by depicting a single head with three faces. At the time it was believed that the panelling was in its original position, suggesting that Jack's house had extended that far from the northern gable. A house of such large proportions was likely to have been built around an inner courtyard. Fortunately the carvings have survived and are at Sudeley Castle, Winchcombe, in Gloucestershire.

The Parish Church of St Nicolas

The church of St Nicolas is first mentioned in the *Hyde Chronicles* of the late 11th century, and it was probably built by Ernulf de Hesdin who granted the church and the Priest's House to Preaux Abbey. This Norman church apparently remained in use until the end of the 15th century, when it was pulled down and rebuilt on a larger scale. There are no remains of the Norman church, but foundations of an earlier building have been unearthed when alterations have taken place, most recently when the boiler room was being enlarged about 1990. The church is a fine and large example of Perpendicular architecture, built between about 1500 and 1532. The latter date appears on the tower, the last part of the building to be completed. Reputedly, Jack of Newbury and his son provided most of the money required to build it.

Whilst the basic structure remains essentially Tudor, there have been some alterations. Those most obvious externally are the embattled parapet around the roof and the pinnacles and turrets of the tower. These were added between 1850 and 1870. During the same period the north chapel was extended to form the vestry and internally fairly extensive changes

St Nicolas' church from a painting by Mrs Everett prior to the mid-19th century alterations. (West Berkshire Museum)

were made to the chancel, including its roof and the chancel arch.

The church is 43 metres long and consists of a chancel with north and south chapels, an aisled nave of five bays with north and south porches, and a western tower. The nave arcades have clustered pillars and richly moulded arches with a hood-mould over. All the pillars are of similar design except the second from the east on the north side which appears to be older than the rest. All the windows are filled with good Perpendicular tracery. The nave and aisle roofs have had to be restored in places and the bosses are carved with various designs, a number having J.S. for John Smallwood. In the nave roof there are moulded tie beams with curved braces whose spandrels are filled with tracery and which spring from the walls resting on modern corbels. The chapels on each side of the chancel are lit by windows of three lights, but the east window of the north chapel was moved to the east end of the vestry when this was built. The east window of the chancel is of six lights.

The reredos and sedilia are modern. Between 1983-1985 restoration work was carried out in the chancel and new choir stalls were commissioned from a master craftsman, Michael Thomas. They are made of English oak and are so designed that they can be moved to allow for the presentation of music and drama in the church. The stained glass windows of the church are mostly 19th century in date.

The tower is of three stages, with octagonal turrets at the corners and there is a peal of ten bells. Below the tower is the brass of Jack of Newbury, 1519, and he is depicted wearing a furred cloak with a belt and pouch, his wife is beside him, and below are his two sons and daughter. There are four later brasses of 1595 and 1641. Also inside the church, although it was mounted on an external wall for many years, is an interesting large stone monument of 1587 to Griffith Curteys and his family. Under one arch is depicted Griffith Curteys who is kneeling and wearing half-armour with a ruff, under the other arch are three wives, and below are six boys and five girls. Griffith Curteys helped to endow the Church Almshouses in 1583. There are other old memorials on the church walls and in the graveyard. The splendid and unusual early Jacobean pulpit was given to the church by Margaret Cross in 1607. The entrances to the churchyard from Bartholomew Street are through two pretty Gothic archways, erected in 1770.

The Reformation

Apart from the suppression of the religious houses and chantries, Newbury did not suffer great persecution at the Reformation. Miles Coverdale, one of Thomas Cromwell's zealous informers, wrote from Newbury that the priests were not energetic enough in carrying out the religious reforms, and about certain popish books he had found; and it is interesting to note that his second letter was carried by 'young Mr Winchcombe'.

The Newbury Martyrs

During the religious persecution in the reign of Queen Mary, Jocelyn Palmer, the young master of Reading Grammar School and former fellow of Magdalen College, Oxford, was tried for heresy and condemned in the parish church, with Thomas Askew and John Gwyn, a weaver. They were burnt at the stake at the Sandpits in 1556, which is believed to be to the west of where The Lamb pub in Enborne Road stands today.

Shaw House and the Dolmans

William Dolman was an important employee of Jack of Newbury, receiving a bequest in the latter's will. It is possibly at this time that Dolman set himself up in business as a cloth merchant. His son, Thomas, acquired such wealth from cloth that he was able to buy estates in the area and further afield. Amongst these was the manor of Shaw, which he purchased in 1554. Some years later he began the building of Shaw House, but died in

Shaw House.

1575 before its completion. This huge house was finished by his second son, Thomas, in 1581. The Dolmans were only one of many families of clothiers who invested their money in land, after all, John Winchcombe II had done so as early as 1540. The cloth trade in Britain was becoming less profitable, whilst rent from property could be increased in line with rising prices. Thomas became a target of the many in Newbury who were put out of work through the decline of the cloth-making trades. It is interesting to note that although a Guild of Weavers is believed to have existed in Newbury at an early date, it was reformed as a Company after receiving a charter from Queen Elizabeth in 1601, during the same period that the trade was declining. It seems that the weavers hoped that having a status similar to the London livery companies might help protect their livelihoods.

The house is the largest Elizabethan mansion in Berkshire and an early example of building in brick in this region. The entrance is of stone, as are quoins, the mullioned windows and other architectural details. It is of two main storeys with a third gabled storey under the tiled roofs. The great staircase has a moulded handrail supported by twisted balusters and there are a number of stone fireplaces throughout the house.

The rooms contain some fine oak panelling of which one panel is of special interest. It can be seen in the room in which King Charles I is reputed to have slept before the Second Battle of Newbury. As the King stood before the window on the morning of the battle he was seen by a Roundhead soldier who shot at him. The bullet missed and became embedded in the panel. The incident is recorded on a brass plate attached to the panel.

The house remained in the hands of the Dolman family until 1724, after which it remained as a private house in the hands of various owners, notably the Duke of Chandos and the Andrews family. Over this time some alterations took place, mainly to the interior, and elaborate gardens with an ornamental canal stretching to the present Robin Hood roundabout were created. During World War II, the house was at first commandeered for use by the army, but after the bombing of the Council Schools in 1943, it was used as a school. In 1945 the owners decided to sell the house and estate and eventually the house was purchased by Berkshire County Council. It remained a mixed school until Park House, at Wash Common, was bought and converted into a secondary boys school, leaving girls only at Shaw. Subsequently it again became a mixed school as Shaw House Comprehensive, by which time a range of additional buildings had been erected to the west of the mansion. In September 1999, a new school was created on the site, following the formal closure of Shaw House and Turnpike Schools and the sale of the latter's premises. This is named Trinity School and additional buildings were provided at Shaw in September 2000, with the Performing Arts block the following Easter. West Berkshire District Council became the education authority in 1998 and inherited from Berkshire County Council the problem of repairing the Elizabethan mansion. In 1982 fairly serious structural faults had been found in the building and it was decided to evacuate it until these had been rectified; temporary buildings were erected in the gardens. Currently, the ancient house is still closed whilst ways are found of raising the substantial funds needed to repair and maintain this important building.

Kendrick's Charity

In 1625 John Kendrick left the then huge sum of £4,000 to the Borough, for the relief of poor clothiers. Part of the sum was to be used to buy 'a commodious house and garden to set poor people on work' and part to provide loans of capital to clothworkers who needed to buy their raw materials or equipment. In the event, the Corporation purchased a site called The Castle with an adjoining acre of meadow and in 1626/7 erected a large building, in three wings, providing all the facilities needed for making and finishing cloth, starting with the raw wool. Unfortunately this did not provide a permanent solution as the market for cloth had declined and much of the cloth remained unsold. The effects of the Civil War, fifteen years later, has confused the situation, but we know that by the end of the 17th century the 'cloth factory' buildings were being put to other uses. One wing of the building remains, in Wharf Street, and forms part of West Berkshire Museum. The meadow was used in the 1720s to form Newbury Wharf including a large basin for barges using the River Kennet Navigation.

Kendrick's generosity to Newbury, and the fact that he was able to leave £7,000 to Reading for similar purposes, indicates the wealth which cloth merchants had been able to amass in the 16th century. But by the

The Old Cloth Hall – now part of West Berkshire Museum.

time of his death the situation had changed, as mentioned above. There had been a decline in the demand for English cloth from the European mainland, which had earlier been a major market. This had arisen from higher prices for wool in England and an increase in the rearing of sheep on the Continent. There was great unemployment and poverty. In 1630, a hungry mob stopped and looted the corn carts going from Newbury to Reading, and, though the ring-leaders were mostly from Speen and Greenham, a number of old Newbury women were punished. Among steps taken to deal with the distress was the closing of 27 alehouses.

Guildhall

In the centre of the Market Place stood the old Guildhall. This may have been built in 1611, but more likely was altered from an earlier structure at that date. The main room was on the first floor, supported on pillars. This provided shelter beneath for some of the market stalls – probably those selling meat or fish. At the north end was a separate building containing smaller rooms and a staircase. This was added to in 1684 to provide prison cells. The town stocks stood outside this building, but the pillory and whipping post were at the southern end of an open balcony which ran along the western side at first floor level. Miscreants receiving these punishments were thus displayed to the populace in the Market Place below. It seems that in the 17th and 18th centuries some meetings of the Borough were held in the main chamber, as were the Quarter Sessions courts. However, the name Guildhall implies that it belonged to a local guild, of which there were several in the town during the Middle Ages, to which the members of the different crafts or trades belonged (see page 21). There was also a Guild of St George, which was open to members of any craft. As the weathervane on the Guildhall was in the form of a dragon, it is tempting to think that the St George's guild was the original owner of the building. An exact replica of the weathervane was put on the 'Cloth Hall' in 1829, two years after the Guildhall was demolished – it remains there today. At the time that the Guildhall was demolished, the town stocks were also destroyed and the Corporation had a portable set made. These stocks of 1827 are preserved in the museum. A little south of the Guildhall stood the market cross, but this has long been demolished.

CHAPTER FOUR

The Civil War

Newbury was a place of considerable strategic importance to both sides in the Civil War, given its proximity to the Royalist headquarters at Oxford and its position on the crucial route between London, the centre of Parliament's power, and the South and West. The 'Great Rebellion', in Lord Clarendon's phrase, produced a complex interplay of loyalties and rivalries. Berkshire was no exception to the general view that 'every county had more or less the civil war within itself'. The strong influence of Puritanism, along with more pragmatic commercial instincts, among the merchants, shopkeepers and tradesmen of the town ensured that Newbury, however, like most other urban communities of the day, sympathised with the Parliamentary cause.

The countryside around Newbury was to be the scene of two particularly bloody engagements, each having crucial if unforeseen consequences for the ultimate outcome of the struggle.

The failure of King Charles to grasp the opportunity afforded by the First Battle of Newbury in September 1643 to win a quick and decisive victory was enormously important. The Royalists had certainly had the better of the conflict in the opening months of the war, but it was imperative that the King should destroy the main Parliamentary army under the command of the Earl of Essex. The longer the war went on the more strained Royalist finances would become and the advantages of the wealth and resources enjoyed by Parliament would shift the balance against the King.

Just such an opportunity to inflict a decisive blow presented itself to the King in September 1643. Royalist successes in the South West had prompted the Earl of Essex to move from his London base to relieve the now isolated garrison at Gloucester, which was the only remaining Parliamentary stronghold between the Bristol Channel and Manchester. Setting out with some 15,000 troops, of which 4,000 were cavalry, on what must be seen as a desperate venture, the Earl of Essex accomplished his first task with little difficulty. The King raised the siege rather than risk being caught between the hostile city and the relieving force. Essex was therefore welcomed by the garrison and entered Gloucester on 8th September in some triumph.

A far harder task however now confronted him – to return to London through enemy held territory. Leaving his heavier ordnance behind, he chose to avoid the circle of Royalist fortresses defending Oxford by marching south as quickly as his baggage train and the condition of roads would allow. At Cirencester he was able to seize a Royalist supply train which helped sustain his tired and hungry men with cartloads of bread and cheese. Three days later, with the Parliamentary army still dangerously strung out between Chiseldon and Aldbourne, the pursuing Royalist cavalry led by Prince Rupert made an attack. This was beaten off with some difficulty and Essex was now determined to put the River Kennet between himself and the King's army. He therefore altered his line of march to cross at Hungerford. Essex appears to have miscalculated the speed of the Royalist advance because he clearly anticipated a welcome billet in Newbury and much needed supplies for his sorely pressed army. His advance party were actually making such arrangements in the town on the afternoon of 19th September when they were rudely interrupted by the advance guard of Rupert's cavalry.

The seriousness of his predicament must have now been clear to Essex. The King's army now lay across his line of march, enjoying the food supplies destined for his near starving and exhausted troops. He had no alternative but to halt his army in the rain sodden fields between the Kennet and the Enborne and await what the morrow might bring. Local tradition has it that the Earl himself spent the night at Bigg's Cottage so perhaps the commander in chief did enjoy the rare luxury of a roof over his head.

The King and his generals on the other hand could be well pleased with having caught up with the enemy. There was some concern that Essex

The Round Hill, so crucial to the Roundheads during the 1st Battle of Newbury. This view faces south. The water tower on Wash Common can be seen on the left.

might slip past in the night but it was a confident Council of War which resolved to confront the Parliamentary army the next day and the King led his forces out of Newbury to bivouac on the flat ground north and east of Skinners Green. Patrols were sent out to reconnoitre the plateau of Wash Common, reporting back that the ground to the south was open and good cavalry country whilst the land to the west was much enclosed and intersected with narrow lanes. What they failed to report was the existence of a further hill to the west – subsequently known as Round Hill – which 'commanded the plain before Newbury where the King's army stood.' This tactical error was to cost the King dear.

After what must have been a miserable and dispiriting night for the Parliamentary forces, with nothing to eat but what they had left in their knapsacks, the army of Essex was on the move before first light on the 20th. The Roundheads must have been heartened, however, by being able to move up from Crockham Heath and Hamstead Park towards the higher ground of Wash Common and take possession of Round Hill without resistance. Essex had been given the chance to take up a strong defensive position which he seized with alacrity. The King's army stood in his path and could have waited for him to take the offensive. Charles' commanders were in no mood for passive resistance. Clarendon describes the over-confidence of the King's young officers 'who unhappily always undervalued the courage of the enemy'. They were determined to take the fight to the Roundheads and the pattern of the battle was dictated by successive Royalist attempts to dislodge Essex's army from its position. The fortunes of the day were to be determined on the slopes of the Round Hill and the fields between the hill and Wash Common Farm.

The First Battle of Newbury

Controversy continues to surround the actual sequence of events of the battle. There are a variety of personal accounts by participants, but rarely do they give an overall view of the battle. It is not even certain how many men fought, though it is known that Parliament had a preponderance of infantry of some 10,000 with 4,000 cavalry while the King could muster a larger cavalry force of about 6,000 with 8,000 infantry. The imbalance between cavalry and infantry was to prove important given the defensive position Essex had taken up in the hedged fields and narrow lanes.

King Charles took personal command of his army although he could rely on the skills of an experienced veteran, Patrick Ruthven, Lord Forth, as his chief of staff. The King's giftedly eccentric and flamboyant nephew Prince Rupert commanded the cavalry which was much more experienced and stood in much higher esteem than their Parliamentary counterparts.

The Earl of Essex on the other hand was desperately short of experienced senior officers – with the particular exception of Sergeant Major General Philip Skippon. It may have been a lack of confidence in his brigade commanders which caused Essex to take personal command of the right wing of the army whilst relying on Skippon to command the left and the reserves.

The Falkland Memorial, erected to commemorate those who fell in the 1st Battle of Newbury.

Essex deployed his army according to the conventions of 17th century warfare, his main body of infantry and artillery in the centre, flanked on either side by cavalry.

The King having deployed his army in similar fashion according to the current disciplines of war, opened hostilities at about 7 am with a series of assaults to dislodge the Roundheads from their positions. This was to set the pattern for the day, the Royalists attacking, the Parliamentarians defending and counter attacking. The pattern, however, frequently degenerated into a confused melee as friend and foe became hopelessly entangled in a desperate struggle for survival.

In a series of cavalry charges and counter charges with heavy losses on both sides, the Parliamentary army's cavalry were eventually driven off the field to play no further part in the battle.

It became clear that the Parliamentary cause now rested with the Roundhead infantry – the outcome of the battle would depend on their tenacity and discipline. It was in the centre on the slopes of Round Hill and the fields near Wash Common Farm that those qualities were tested to the full. The Royalists' cavalry brigade and infantry managed to dislodge the defending infantry and gain a footing on the hill – at the cost of the life of Lord Falkland and a hundred members of his own regiment, who were slain in their attempts to breach the hedges.

This proved a critical point of the battle because Skippon threw in the London trained bands to stabilize his crumbling centre. The five regiments of trained bands, some 5,000 strong, mainly crop-headed apprentices conscripted from the London crafts and trades, had been held in reserve, but were now to bear the brunt of the Royalist onslaught. Moving to their position to secure the top of Skinners Green Lane, they came under murderous fire from the main Royalist battery. Roundhead big guns were eventually positioned and a fierce cannonade ensued – but Rupert was impatient to sweep the dogged trained bands away and hurled repeated assaults at them. But they stood resolute and firm. Had the Royalist infantry followed the example of their cavalry the day might have ended differently.

The killing ground on the Wash ridge and the high ground of the plateau continued to be hotly disputed until nightfall. As darkness descended and fighting petered out the Roundheads were still in possession of their ground. Both sides had committed all their troops, fighting had continued all day and men must simply have slumped down and slept exhausted on the bloody field. Nothing appeared to have been resolved. The King's army still barred the road to London and Essex had to steel his army for a final desperate effort to break through. His relief the next morning to discover the Royalist army had gone must therefore have been considerable!

Controversy still surrounds the King's decision to abandon the field. The Council of War he had called in the evening had been divided and the King took the momentous decision to return to Oxford on the advice of his more cautious officers alarmed by their heavy losses and concerned by their depleted reserves of gunpowder. Thus it was that Essex found the road to the east unopposed. The plan to annihilate Essex's army and bring a swift end to the war had failed – and with it the King's best chance of regaining his kingdom.

The Earl of Essex had halted the tide of Royalist success and ensured the survival of the Parliamentary cause for better days. This had been bought at high cost on Newbury's fields.

The greatest individual loss to the King's cause was undoubtedly Viscount Falkland, his Secretary of State. Tradition has it that his corpse was retrieved from the field and taken to the house at Falkland Garth which still survives. His sacrifice is commemorated in the Falkland Memorial which stands at the junction of Essex Street and Andover Road. Raised in 1878 it pays tribute to the memory of Falkland and the men who fell fighting in the King's cause. A simpler but more even handed inscription is to be found on the burial mounds of Wash Common to those who fell in the tragedy of the Civil War. The mounds themselves are unlikely to contain dead from the battle as they are reputed to date from the Bronze Age. They may well have provided convenient cover from the main battery of Royalist cannon, an emplacement for which was discovered in the construction of the last house in the aptly named Battery End.

The visitor to the battlefield today will find some difficulty in retracing locations and events. Much of the southern part of the field is now completely covered by a housing estate. The centre of the battle in the area of Skinners Green, Round Hill and the fields around Wash Common Farm is in private ownership and access without permission is restricted to the public roads and footpaths. But it is possible to gain an impression of the terrain through gaps in the surviving hawthorn hedges – the remnants of those small enclosed fields which served the Roundhead pikemen and musketeers so well. Such is the tranquillity of the scene, however, that it requires a quantum leap of the imagination to conceive the carnage and mayhem which turned the tide of history on that fateful day in 1643.

The Second Battle of Newbury

Such are the fortunes of war, that by the time of the Second Battle of Newbury in October 1644 it was Parliament that held the upper hand and was in a position to inflict a crushing defeat on the King's forces. In the autumn of 1644 the King returned from military triumphs in the West Country to relieve the beleaguered garrisons of Donnington Castle, Banbury and Basing House.

Parliament may well have interpreted this move as part of a plan to attack London and so at last decided to concentrate their main armies, reinforced by London trained bands, to challenge the King who was reported to have moved to Newbury. Estimates vary as to the total of Parliamentary forces, 19,000 is a minimum calculation and there may have been substantially more.

This large force which assembled near Thatcham on 26th October had no overall commander. The Earl of Essex had become ill and retired to bed in Reading so responsibility was shared by two chief commanders – Sir William Waller and the Earl of Manchester.

The King had taken up a strong defensive position based on a triangle of strongpoints at Shaw House, Donnington Castle and Speen Village, but his forces numbered no more than 9,000. This gave the Parliamentarians a numerical superiority of more than two to one. They seemed to have been presented with a golden opportunity to destroy the King's army and end the war.

Emboldened by their numerical superiority, the Parliamentary commanders devised an ambitious strategy. The plan was for Waller to take a large force by night, march round the north of the Royalist position and attack the enemy in the rear from the west. This would be co-ordinated by Manchester who would attack from the east as soon as gunfire was heard from the west. The Royalists would thus be 'caught between hammer and anvil' as long as the attacks could occur simultaneously.

Such are the vagaries of war that the plan and the reality are often different. And so it was to prove.

Waller set off on his seven mile march to Speen on the evening of Saturday the 26th with some 12,000 troops, Skippon commanding the infantry, Sir William Balfour and Lt General Oliver Cromwell the cavalry. They moved north via Hermitage and then west through Chieveley. At least part of the night was spent at North Heath. In the morning there was a skirmish with a Royalist outpost at Boxford before they advanced via Wickham Heath and Stockcross to deploy their main attack against Speen. That Waller was unable to deploy until about 3 o'clock in the afternoon of Sunday 27th gives some measure of the difficulties of moving large numbers of men along narrow 17th century roads.

It would seem that the Royalists were taken by surprise as most of the cavalry were away foraging. Sir Philip Skippon's men stormed the fortifications and after some fierce fighting were in possession of Speen and the Royalists were in full retreat towards Donnington and Newbury. With Speen secured Waller was now in a position to develop his attack from the west. At about 4 o'clock the cavalry brigades were launched against the Cavaliers, Balfour to the right between Speen and the Kennet, Cromwell to the left between Speen and Donnington. The Royalists responded in kind to these two great cavalry charges with the King very much in the thick of things. In the hard fighting that followed Balfour made little headway and Cromwell and his Ironsides even less.

But crucially Manchester delayed his attack until well after Skippon had wrested control of Speen. It may be that it was difficult to distinguish the gunfire from Speen from the desultory bombardment that had been going on most of the day. For whatever reason the planned assault on the Shaw House sector came at least an hour too late.

Lord Astley (who as Sir Jacob had commanded the Royalist infantry in the First Battle of Newbury and had since received his baronetcy) had prepared the defences of Shaw House 'with great contrivance'. Astley shared his command of the defence with Colonel George Lisle and it was against a small but well organised and well positioned body of men that Manchester eventually launched his major assault of some 3,000 infantry supported by 1,200 cavalry. As the Roundheads came down Clay Hill their psalm singing was met with withering volleys of fire. Fighting was desperately fierce and the Roundheads suffered heavy casualties – perhaps as many as 500 killed. The attack was eventually abandoned and the Parliamentarians withdrew in some confusion. The skill of Lord Astley and the courage of his men had held the Shaw position against the odds of at least 3 to 1, but the particular hero of the defence seems to have been George Lisle. Having led by example throughout the action, as the light faded he stripped off his buff coat so his men could recognise his white shirt in the gloom and smoke – and according to a contemporary broadsheet was taken by the Roundheads to be a witch!

So as the night fell the Parliamentary commanders had little to be pleased with. The attack on Shaw had been repulsed and although Speen had been taken, Waller had been unable to break the Royalists from the west. They had lost perhaps 1,000 casualties and inflicted far less on the enemy.

The King, however, was in an untenable position between the Roundhead forces and so having withdrawn from the field at dusk to Donnington Castle, he departed for Bath, leaving Prince Maurice and Lord Astley to organise the retreat. This they did, taking their guns and wounded to the shelter of Donnington Castle, without any interference from the Parliamentarians.

As a result of the missed opportunities and poor performance at the Second Battle of Newbury, there came a searching assessment of Parliament's generals which resulted in the Self Denying Ordinance promoted by Cromwell which called for the resignation of existing generals and a restructuring of command. What emerged was the New Model Army under Sir Thomas Fairfax which was to prove the instrument of Parliament's ultimate victory.

Thus unlikely as it seemed at the time, 'Second Newbury' was to signal the end of the King's military hopes which were to be shattered finally on the fields of Naseby.

Donnington Castle

No mention of Newbury in the Civil War would be complete without some reference to the epic siege of Donnington Castle. At the time of the Civil War the castle was owned by John Packer, whose sympathies were with Parliament. Given the crucial strategic position commanding the crossroads of the main routes north-south and east-west, the King was determined to have it under a loyal custodian. Therefore before returning to Oxford after the First Battle of Newbury in 1643, he installed a garrison of the Earl Rivers regiment, some 200 foot, 25 cavalry and 4 cannon, under Sir John Boys. This gallant commander was to prove more than worthy of his sovereign's trust in him.

Around the castle Sir John constructed elaborate diamond shaped earthwork defences for his artillery, in the style of the 'star fort' fortifications of contemporary warfare. These impressive defences, though much overgrown, can still be seen.

Donnington Castle – a besieger's view.

The castle was therefore well prepared to meet an assault by a Parliamentary force under General Middleton when it arrived in July 1644, to begin a siege which was to last for some twenty months. Having rejected surrender terms Boys proceeded to beat off an assault and then stage a sally which inflicted over a hundred casualties on the Roundheads. The assault became more serious in September, however, with the arrival of heavy siege artillery which in a constant twelve day bombardment did serious damage to the fabric of the castle but still did not prevent the Cavaliers from mounting another counter-attack and driving the besiegers back with great loss.

The relief of the castle had been one of the King's main objectives when he arrived in Newbury in October 1644. Donnington inevitably became one of the key positions during the Second Battle and Boys and the men of the Earl Rivers regiment added to their exemplary service. Boys was given responsibility for the artillery and was wounded after the battle as the Roundhead siege closed in again. According to Lord Clarendon it is at this point, with the Roundhead army massed before him, that Boys

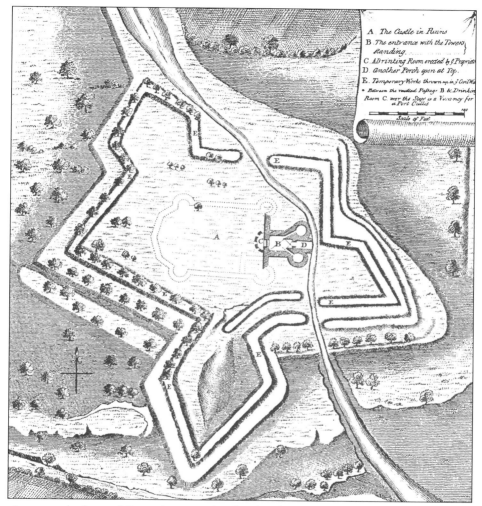

A ground plan of Donnington Castle clearly showing the defensive earthworks constructed by the Royalist defenders.

responded to the threat that failure to surrender would leave no stone standing with the famous retort 'He was not bound to repair it: however, he would, by God's help, keep the ground.'

The fact that the King returned to Donnington to pick up his artillery and defied them to give battle must have added to the Roundheads' exasperation. The King stayed overnight with his champion at Donnington before bidding what was to be a final farewell. The siege was to go on but there were to be no more serious assaults. Boys eventually received a personal order to surrender from the King who was about to give himself up to the Scottish army at Southwell.

So it was that in April 1646 Sir John Boys marched his gallant defenders out of the castle's ruins, with colours flying and drums beating – the full military honours which he and they so richly deserved.

Today the imposing Gate House still stands, bearing the repairs of cannon and mortar damage and the visitor can still walk the earthwork ramparts with the spirit of Sir John Boys and his Cavaliers.

The Aftermath of War

The Civil War had brought great distress and even ruin to many of the Newbury people. Houses were destroyed, livestock was stolen and crops were laid waste, while clothiers suffered losses which they could ill afford when their convoys were attacked and rifled.

Both Royalists and Roundheads shared equal blame. Neither party showed any respect for law and order if they were looking for booty.

Further distress was caused in 1653 when one hundred Dutch prisoners were quartered in the town during the war with Holland.

In 1655 Newbury was alarmed by the arrival of troops under the command of Cromwell's brother-in-law, Major General Disbrowe. They were on their way to the West Country to suppress a Royalist uprising led by two Wiltshire Colonels, John Penruddock of Compton Chamberlayne, and Colonel Grove of Chisenbury. The ill fated rebellion led to the execution of John Kensey, a Newbury surgeon, who met his death at Salisbury, and the displacement of a number of Newbury officials who had supported the cause. Among them was Gabriel Cox, formerly Mayor, and then Town Clerk, who later accused his successor of destroying the town records.

CHAPTER FIVE

1660–1800

In spite of its Puritan tendencies during the Civil War, Newbury greeted the restoration of the monarchy with tremendous enthusiasm. On the 29th May 1660, bonfires blazed in and around the town, the church bells were rung for two days, the corporation feasted, and the townspeople were treated to free wine, ale and cakes.

Three years later King Charles II came to Newbury, accompanied by his Queen, Catherine of Braganza, his brother, James, Duke of York, and his nephew, Prince Rupert. After being received by the Mayor and dignitaries of the town the King was congratulated upon his restoration to the throne and presented with a purse of gold. The royal party were the guests of Sir Thomas Dolman of Shaw House. After dinner the King, together with his brother and nephew, visited the battlefields.

In 1664/5 Charles presented his new charter to the town thus strengthening the Royalist element. Some of the former prosperity returned, and the Company of Clothiers and Hatters used to parade after the service from the church to the Globe Inn, with the 'town music' in front, then the men, and lastly the women, all in their best clothes.

The Plague 1665

Unfortunately, such pleasures were rudely interrupted when the plague reached Newbury from London in spite of all precautions taken by the town's authorities. It was not unknown in the town, but this time it was so severe that everyone was fearful of becoming a victim of the terrible disease. There was no time to record the number of dead but tradition has it that they were taken from the town at nightfall for burial on the open downs. A horn or trumpet was sounded to warn villagers to stay indoors as the tragic procession passed along the country roads.

Almshouses

The plight of the poor weighed on the consciences of the more prosperous and several almshouses were established between 1671 and 1790 by Thomas Pearce, Francis Coxedd, Philip Jemmet, Thomas Hunt, Benjamin Robinson and John Kimber. The largest of these was Raymonds' Almshouses, established before 1676 by Philip Jemmet and further endowed by his son-in-law and daughter, Sir Jonathan and Lady Raymond. Jemmet's original foundation was for 12 almspeople, and the number was later increased to 22. The almshouses were at first in the old building on the west side of Argyle Road, but they were moved to the east side of Newtown Road in 1796 with a later range north of Derby Road.

Religion

There were already a number of Nonconformists in Newbury at the beginning of the Civil War, and the sympathies of many of the churchgoers were with the Puritans. This led to riots over the election of a churchwarden, in 1664, but threats of calling in soldiers brought a temporary truce. A Presbyterian, William Milton, was the ringleader, and when he was being questioned, his followers rose and attempted to rescue him. But the troop prevented this, and Milton was sent to London with a number of others for trial. After this event, the number of practising Nonconformists was given as only 40. The Quakers had become established in the town by 1683, and their meeting house stood back from Bartholomew Street on the west side. Now they meet on Sunday mornings at No 1 Highfield Avenue. The Presbyterians moved their meeting house from Bartholomew Street to the Waterside Chapel in 1697, and this date was upon the wall. This old chapel was most picturesque with its mellow red-brick walls, moulded cornice and gabled roofs. In 1960, owing to disrepair, it unfortunately had to be demolished. The Independents built their first chapel in 1717, and other denominations also had early chapels.

The Great Frost

Weather conditions are the subject of conversation in every age. In the winter of 1683/4 it was the severe frost that was the talking point. It started in Newbury at the beginning of December 1683 and continued for the next thirteen weeks. Ice was reported to be eighteen inches thick in places and the Kennet was frozen over. Deer and sheep were killed, trees felled, and giant oaks were split by the severity of the frost. The plight of the people can be imagined. When the thaw came the floods brought further devastation and fears that the whole town would be flooded were only allayed by prompt action by the authorities and the townspeople.

A Royal Visit

In 1686 King James II came to the town and was formally received by the Mayor and Corporation but his visit did not arouse the same enthusiasm as that of his brother, possibly because the town could not afford to provide lavish entertainments for a somewhat unpopular monarch. The following year Newbury was involved with the King again. It was the fair of St Simon and St Jude that was the cause of the trouble. Ever since the fair was granted by Queen Elizabeth it had been held in the town but in 1687 it was moved to Wash Common by order of the Mayor and Corporation as lords of the manor. However, Newburians were not pleased and complaints were made to the Crown authorities with the result that the Mayor, Mr Francis Cox, was summoned before King James II and his Privy Council when it was ordered that the fair should return to the town with a special fair for sheep in the West Fields.

Queen Anne

Queen Anne was accorded a greater welcome than her father when she visited Newbury in 1703. She was received 'with all imaginable joy, honour, and triumph.' She was the guest of Mr Thomas Dolman of Shaw House. He was subsequently knighted for his hospitality when he visited St James' in November of the same year.

Newbury Market Place as it would have appeared at the turn of the
19th century; by the artist Thomas Rowlandson (1756–1827).
The Guildhall in the centre was pulled down in 1827.

The Newbury Skirmish

The town was not in such a joyous mood three years later when a military pressgang was on hand, and a riot, called the Newbury Skirmish, took place. Two sergeants were sent to apprehend an idle fellow named John Pinfold but friends came to his help, one of the sergeants was knocked down, and he was rescued. Soldiers arrived on the scene, and he was recaptured to be again rescued. Pinfold was once more seized, and was being led away when the angry mob attacked the soldiers and a sergeant was killed. The constable and watchman had sided with the mob, but some officers came to the rescue and many of the rioters fell.

Education

Apart from the Grammar School, there were few facilities for education at the beginning of the 18th century. Francis Coxedd had left a large sum of money to be used, partly for almshouses and partly for educating children. In 1706, the Corporation used some of this money to endow a charity school for 20 poor boys under the name Kendricks School. Richard Cowslade added to this foundation in 1715, and other charity schools followed. Through the benefactions of John and Frances West, Newbury has been privileged since 1728 to send children to be educated at Christ's Hospital, one of the best public schools in the country. Special grants are also available from the same bequest. The scheme has been varied both in regard to administration and the number of places. Boys and girls of Newbury still value the privilege of attending the now co-educational Christ's Hospital at Horsham, West Sussex.

The Town Hall

The Town Hall, or Mansion House, was erected between the years 1740 and 1742. The basement of the building was fitted with an extensive and costly cooking apparatus for the Mayor's Inauguration Dinner, and other functions which took place on the first floor. The hall was built over open arches and the 'shambles' underneath were used by stallholders for the sale of meat, butter, cheese, poultry and other country wares.

Roads in the 18th Century

The many ancient roads which met at Newbury have already been described. By the 17th century roads throughout England were in a very poor state. In theory parishioners had to give three or four days free work for the maintenance of high roads which passed through their parish. In practice no one likes to work for nothing and maintenance was skimped. A solution to the problem was found by groups of landowners and other wealthy people agreeing to finance the improvement and resurfacing of roads in return for the right to charge each user. For each stretch of road an Act of Parliament was required to authorise what became known as turnpike trusts. This all took many years, partly due to opposition from users who didn't wish to pay for improvements and from others with vested interests. For instance there were 12 Acts passed between 1707 and 1756 for improvements to the complete length of· the road from London to Bath (via Chippenham) – and this for one of the country's busiest roads!

Neither did the improvements brought in by the turnpike trustees bring the roads to a standard we would consider acceptable. In 1767 a

The old Toll House at the junction of Oxford Road and Bath Road. It was demolished in 1950.

writer to the *Reading Mercury*, reporting on the road, referred to muddiness, flooding and narrow stretches, especially the situation at Ham Mills (near B&Q) where it was dangerous for two coaches to pass as it was narrow and had ditches on each side, one very deep. It was not until the 1820s and 30s that the real improvements to road structure developed by Telford and McAdam came into use and consistent cambers and drainage provisions were also incorporated into the design of the country's roads. Users were stopped at toll gates and charged varying rates, on a published scale of charges, according the perceived wear they would cause. On the Bath road through Newbury there was a gate west of Thatcham (near where Tull Road now leaves the A4), at the junction with Oxford Road at Speenhamland and at Halfway (one mile before the Kintbury turn). The road from Andover to Oxford had gates at Wash Water, Wash Common (adjoining The Gun public house), and adjacent to The Castle Inn at Donnington. The gates at Wash Water and Donnington were the last to remain in use in the area, closing as late as 1880.

Because Turnpike Road at Shaw is so called, there is some confusion over the route of the road into Newbury. It followed more or less the same line as the present A4, though it is possible that the route via Shaw may have been used on occasions when the main road was impassable. Turnpike Road was thus named in 1934 as it led from or to the former toll house – which stood until 1964.

Coaching and Inns

The town of Bath discovered a renewed interest in its renowned hot springs towards the end of the 17th century. More people had time to indulge in remedies for their ailments and the waters of Bath (and other spas) were thought efficacious for health – whether through drinking them, bathing or having water pumped over the afflicted part of the body! Whilst there was adequate accommodation for visitors, there was only limited means of entertainment to while away the hours when 'cures' were not being taken. But, by the beginning of the 18th century, additional facilities such as the Assembly Rooms had been built and, of equal importance, Beau Nash became Master of Ceremonies of the resort. He organised entertainments and brought in rules of conduct, such as banning

The Pelican Inn, from a painting of around 1835.

the wearing of swords (which he thought encouraged duels) or wearing of riding boots indoors. Although most visitors were socially superior to Nash they accepted his restraints as they appreciated the order he brought and the excellence of the entertainments he provided. As the 18th century developed, more and more people, and from a wider stratum of society, came to visit Bath and stayed for longer and longer periods of time. Much new building took place to provide semi-permanent accommodation for the really wealthy and houses or rooms to rent for others. Bath developed into a pleasure resort, rather than simply a place visited to improve one's health.

But what has this to do with Newbury? The answer is: quite a lot. As mentioned above, the country's roads were in poor condition and The Great Bath Road, with all its defects, was used by virtually everyone travelling to Bath from the south-east corner of Britain. The coach journey from the capital to Bath took two long days travelling: many stops were needed as well as the slow speed of the coaches. Almost exactly halfway between the two was Newbury, or, more precisely, part of the parish of Speen which abutted the northern end of Northbrook Street and was called

Speenhamland. By the mid-18th century there were nine inns between Shaw Road and Oxford Road, plus The Castle Inn opposite Speen Lane. The Kings Arms was built about 1700 as an inn, but others such as the Lamb and Flag, The Angel, Cross Keys (later rebuilt) and Chequers probably originated in the medieval era. As mentioned earlier, Newbury had long been an important town on Britain's road network and would have provided for travellers. One of the best-known inns on Bath Road was the George and Pelican, its name usually shortened to The Pelican. Its buildings still stand at Broadway and stretch along London Road. The eastern end of this range formed the entrance to The Pelican stables, which had accommodation for 300 horses! It was famed for its food, but appears to have been expensive as in the mid-18th century, a famous actor of the period, James Quinn, reputedly scratched a verse on one of its windows:

> The famous inn at Speenhamland that stands below the hill,
> may well be called the Pelican from its enormous bill.

Not only did these inns, the wants of their clients and provision of horses provide much direct employment, but it seems likely that the number of travellers led to the development of a significant clock and watch making industry. There were over a hundred clockmakers in Newbury, Speen and Shaw between 1680 and 1840, some of them producing very high quality work.

Although there had been visiting theatre companies in Newbury from at least the 1780s, when a purpose-built theatre was erected in 1802, it was built at Speenhamland, at the north end of a square to the west of the Bacon Arms. It seems that this was because of the potential custom of travellers spending the night nearby.

Whilst the concentration of inns was in Speenhamland, there were others in the town and, of course, coaches running on the north-south routes. The principal inns were The Jack, in Northbrook Street (Marks & Spencer's is on its site), The Globe on the south side of the bridge (where Lloyds Bank now stands) and The White Hart in the Market Place. The latter was the base of the 'Flying Coach' started in 1752 by John Clark and so called because of the speed at which it travelled to London – it took a mere twelve hours! To achieve this no passengers were carried outside and only four inside; they could take only hand baggage, other luggage had to follow by a slower coach or wagon.

Mail Coaches

From the 17th century there had been a system of mail being carried by postboys on horseback on six routes leading from London, with inns every ten or fifteen miles providing fresh horses and dealing with the mail for their town or along routes leading from it. This system was modified, with independent contractors paying an annual fee to the Post Office and taking responsibility for delivering the mails, especially on the cross-country routes, ie those not going through London. But in 1784 a more fundamental change took place, starting on 2nd August, with an experimental fast coach with an armed guard, carrying the mails from London to Bath and Bristol. This proved a success with mail being delivered more quickly and reliably. Fresh horses and the mails had to be ready for when the coach stopped and they were also exempt from tolls. The turnpike keeper had to raise the bar, following a blast of the horn from

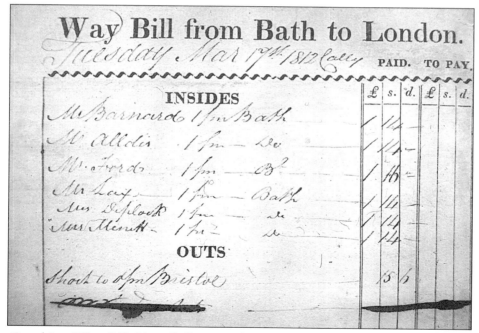

Coaching Way Bill (detail) from Bath to London in 1812. The fare was £1.14.0 from Bath to London, two shillings more from Bristol, but only 15s 6d return if one travelled outside! (West Berkshire Museum)

the approaching coach, and equally all other traffic had to pull aside to allow the mails to pass without delay. Within three years the system was in use throughout England and Scotland. Initially, contractors supplied what conveyances and horses they had available, but by the end of the century a new design of coach with black and red livery was introduced. The standard of coachmen eventually improved, with the new generation trained, dressed in smart coats and beaver hats and experts in driving a coach and four. The guard was responsible for the time-keeping of the coach and security of the mail. Should the coach be delayed, by accident or winter weather, he had to take one horse and do his best to deliver the mail on time. The mail coaches also carried passengers who were prepared to pay for a rapid journey; four inside and two outside.

Coachmen

Whilst some of the old coachmen may have been a little careless of their duties and some overfond of strong drink, at the height of the coaching era (1780–1840) the best coachmen were an elite class of workers. They needed to be literate and numerate to keep account of the fares of their passengers and fees for parcels carried on their journeys as well as expert drivers. In the early 19th century many of them chose to live in the newly-built houses of Shaw Road.

Exciting and picturesque it may appear when we look back on the coaching days, but in the bad weather the conditions were atrocious and much hardship was suffered by both passengers and horses. Schedules were difficult to maintain and complaints were many as can be gathered from an inscription on the gravestone of a coachman who was buried in Speen churchyard:

In memory of James Murray
Late Bath Coachman
who died 20th May 1796
aged 46 years.

Tho' while on earth I did remain
I was reproached and scorned by men
But now am numbered with the saints
And saf'd of all my long complaints.

Canals

The River Kennet from Newbury to Reading, where it joined the Thames, was made navigable for sailing barges in 1723. This was done by dredging sections of the river, cutting new channels to reduce the length of the meandering natural course and building locks – some to avoid the many watermills along the river. A large basin for loading and unloading was excavated at Newbury and storage buildings provided, to form Newbury Wharf. The whole of this substantial piece of engineering was overseen by John Hore, whose family operated Ham Mills, where the Lambourn joined the Kennet. Today, it seems strange to expend so much effort to avoid seventeen miles of road, but in the early 18th century the condition of the roads meant that especially for heavy or bulky goods the investment was worthwhile. The waterway seems to have found rapid success, with manufacturers and traders from Salisbury, Devizes, Chippenham, Bath and Bristol loading their products onto barges at Newbury for transit to London and other towns in-between. A wide range of goods, including foods, raw materials, stone and coal were carried back from the capital. Newbury became a busy inland port. Whilst the storage buildings of the Granary still survive, as does the home/office of the proprietor of the wharf, Wharf House (formerly Kendrick House), nothing can now be seen of the basin. This originally left the River Kennet just east of the bridge which now carries the A339 over the river and ran almost to Wharf House.

Kennet and Avon Canal

The success of the Kennet Navigation led to calls for it to be extended westwards. Eventually work was begun at Newbury, in 1794, to construct a canal linking the Kennet Navigation with the River Avon Navigation, at Bath. Work was completed in 1810 (though lengths had been in use earlier) providing an inland waterway link between the ports of Bristol and London. The work was planned and supervised by the eminent engineer John Rennie and cost £1,072,000.

Trade declined later in the 19th century, but a small level of use continued until 1950 when it was suddenly closed following the collapse of a lock. A court case, with an appeal to the House of Lords, ensued – in the name of John Gould Waterways, of Newbury. This was successful, but it took many years of fund-raising by the Kennet & Avon Canal Trust, local authorities and others to finance its restoration and re-opening to traffic. HM The Queen officially reopened the canal at Devizes in August 1990. John and Wyn Gould were amongst the VIP guests. John had earlier been awarded the MBE for his work for the canal's restoration over many years. Bath stone for the restoration of Windsor Castle after the fire of 1992 was an early commercial use of the re-opened waterway.

Newbury Bridge pre-dates the canal and therefore there is no provision for a towpath. This created some difficulty for the owners of horse-drawn boats travelling downstream, as it is a relatively short distance from Newbury lock to the bridge and between them a channel of the river rejoins the canal. Boats leaving the lock needed to gain momentum quickly so as not to be pushed off course when heading for the narrow bridge. Long ropes needed to be used and horses towing boats had to turn sharply left into a tunnel beneath 105, Northbrook Street (adjacent to the bridge) whilst pulling hard. The tow-ropes cut grooves into the brickwork which can still be seen. There must have been a tendency for owners to make their horses continue pulling whilst they crossed Northbrook Street, as there was a notice on the cottage which used to stand at the side of the lock forbidding this dangerous practice! To haul boats upstream through the bridge provided a different problem. Boats had to moor just below the bridge and the towing rope had to be floated back through it, using a special float kept at the lock.

Newbury Bridge/the Kennet Bridge

The views of the 18th century bridge from the riverside are picturesque and it has been painted and photographed throughout its life. For centuries there had been a wooden bridge over the Kennet at the south end of Northbrook Street, and it is recorded that this bridge needed repair in the 14th century. The old bridge had shops upon it. In 1623 the wooden bridge collapsed and was rebuilt but the new bridge was swept away in the flood of 1726, when another wooden bridge was constructed. The present bridge was begun in 1769 and finished three years later. It was

Kennet Bridge c1906.

Newbury from West Mills; a watercolour by Victor M. Corden c1910.

designed by James Clarke and cost over £700. The bridge is of a single span, built of brick with stone dressings and balustrades although two further arches support the carriageway as it rises each side. These arches once provided storage areas for the adjacent properties. At each of the four corners of the main span were once free-standing structures, with stone arches supported by pilasters. Three of these have been incorporated into the adjoining premises to form windows or doorways. It is thought that originally, as well as being decorative features of the bridge, these may have been small shops or kiosks – perhaps selling the trout or crayfish for which Newbury was renowned. The strength of the bridge was proved during the 1939-45 war when vehicles and tanks of the heaviest types were perpetually crossing. However, the foundations of the bridge had been strengthened with a concrete inverted arch in the 1920s, after it was discovered that the tops of the wooden piles which supported the main arch had rotted away.

Bread Riots

As travellers passed through Newbury they probably saw an apparently busy town and failed to notice the plight of those whose lives were made miserable by the decline in trade in general, and the cloth trade in particular, as years of war took their toll on the national economy.

In 1766 a large number of poor people assembled in the Market Place on an August market day to demonstrate against the high price of bread. They upset sacks of corn, butchers' and other traders' stalls, so that everything was scattered in the streets. They wrecked the houses of two unpopular tradesmen, and the butchers' and provisions shops were raided. To pacify the mob the bakers reduced the price of bread by 2d with promises of a further reduction; but the crowd then marched to Shaw Mill, where they did great damage and threw the flour into the river. Other mills were then raided, and one man was killed and several people were injured. The arrival of troops prevented further disorder, and several arrests were made, two of the ringleaders being transported. The Corporation of Newbury made good the damage which had been done.

Cloth Manufacture

In the last half of the century the woollen trade had almost, but not entirely, been reduced to the making of shalloon, an inferior type of cloth used for sail cloth, floors, sacking, and the lining of men's coats of inferior type. Another way in which it was used can be seen in the West Berkshire Museum where is displayed a pall cloth used by the Weavers' Company. This company made a last effort to revive the trade by advertising that they had agreed to disannul their powers and their right to settle the price which any person in the trade should give for making any kinds of goods. They promised free liberty for strangers to come into the town and manufacture silks, muslins, cotton, linen, worsted and other cloths without any interference from the Company of Weavers. A silk weaving factory, with workers cottages, was erected in London Road, just east of the present Robin Hood roundabout, and survived in business for two or three decades. The Weavers' Company set forth the amenities of the town in the final paragraph of their advertisement:

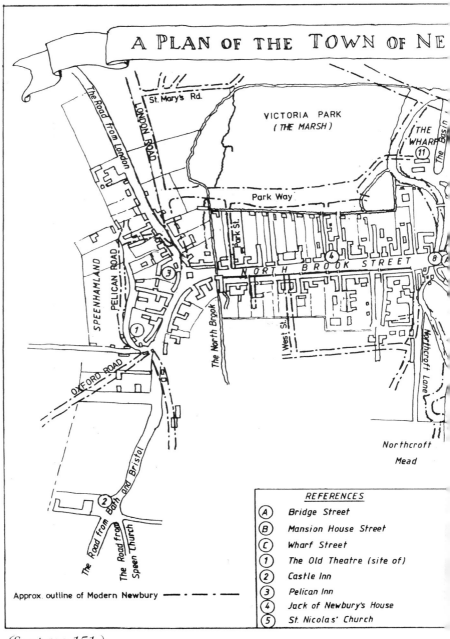

A PLAN OF THE TOWN OF NE

REFERENCES

Ⓐ	Bridge Street
Ⓑ	Mansion House Street
Ⓒ	Wharf Street
①	The Old Theatre (site of)
②	Castle Inn
③	Pelican Inn
④	Jack of Newbury's House
⑤	St. Nicolas' Church

Approx. outline of Modern Newbury — · — · — · —

(See page 151.)

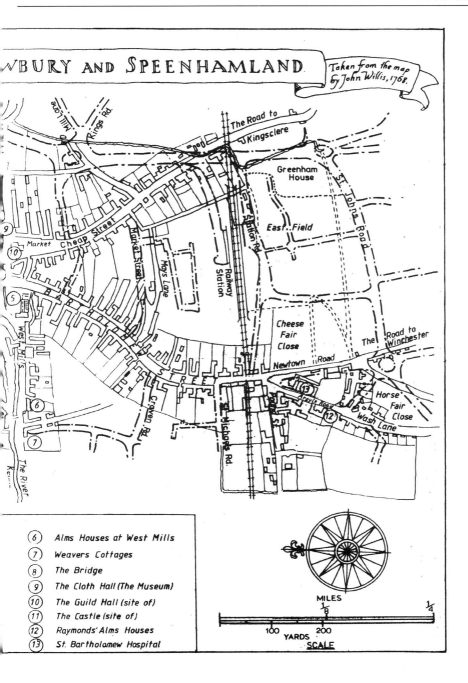

WBURY AND SPEENHAMLAND.

Taken from the map by John Willis, 1768.

The Road to Kingsclere

Greenham House

East Field

Railway Station

Cheese Fair Close

The Road to Winchester

Newtown Road

Horse Fair Close

Wash Lane

Kings Rd.

Mill Lane

Market

Cheap Street

Market Street

Mays Lane

Station Rd.

St. Johns Road

West Mills

Craven Rd.

St. Nicholas Rd.

The River Kennet

Argyle Road

⑥	Alms Houses at West Mills
⑦	Weavers Cottages
⑧	The Bridge
⑨	The Cloth Hall (The Museum)
⑩	The Guild Hall (site of)
⑪	The Castle (site of)
⑫	Raymonds' Alms Houses
⑬	St. Bartholomew Hospital

MILES
$\frac{1}{8}$
$\frac{1}{4}$

100   200
YARDS
SCALE

75

'Newbury is a town well supplied with water and an extraordinary good market to supply its inhabitants with every accommodation that can make life comfortable, and it is well situated to carry on an extensive trade, having an easy conveyance to and from London by the River Kennet.'

It was of no use, the cloth trade was passing to the north of England where new machinery was being set up in the fast growing manufacturing towns. Only John Coxeter of Greenham Mills made a bid to stem the exodus of the remaining Newbury weavers to more prosperous territories, but his story is told in the next chapter.

Speenhamland Act

Although the title given to this event implies that it was an Act of Parliament, this was not the case, it was simply a local scheme that became widely adopted in southern and eastern England. The Berkshire magistrates met at the George and Pelican, Speenhamland, on 6th May 1795. This was at a time when there were high prices and low wages, giving rise to much poverty. The magistrates devised a scale of relief to be provided from the poor rates, based upon the current price of bread. The good intentions of the magistrates failed as it encouraged employers to underpay their employees, knowing that they would receive additional benefits from the parish. It demoralised the recipients and also led to an increased demand on ratepaying parishioners due to the great number of families applying for poor relief.

---CHAPTER SIX---

The Nineteenth Century

Newbury Theatre

As an added inducement to travellers to spend the night in Newbury as they journeyed from London to Bath, a theatre was opened in Speenhamland in 1802. It stood back from Oxford Street conveniently close to the best coaching inns. The theatre was first operated by Henry Thornton who had previously run a theatre in Northcroft Lane.

Under the management of Mr Edward Barnett, his son in law, whose company also visited Reading and other leading towns, the great actors and actresses of the early 19th century performed in Newbury. They included Edmund Keen, John Philip Kemble, Mrs Jordan, Miss Bruton and several others, so that in addition to the visitors, the townspeople were able to enjoy first class entertainment at their local theatre. Regular visits by Barnett's company ceased about 1833. Ten years later it was taken on by Mr E.T. Holmes and his company for two seasons, but with only small success. The theatre finally closed soon afterwards and was put to other uses until it was demolished in 1976.

Jubilee of King George III

In 1810 the town was in festive mood as it celebrated the Golden Jubilee of King George III. After day-time celebrations, which moved a local journal to report that Newbury 'in its arrangements on this occasion has surpassed itself and set an example worthy of the imitation of every part of the kingdom', over 400 people attended a ball at the Mansion House in the presence of the Margravine of Anspach of Benham Place.

The Newbury Coat

The following year was the time when John Coxeter made the headlines. Having introduced machinery into his mill at Greenham he boasted to Sir John Throckmorton of Buckland that within twenty four hours he could take a coat off Sir John's back, reduce it to wool, and turn it back into a coat again. Obviously, the baronet was reluctant to relinquish his coat but he asked Mr Coxeter if it would be possible to sit down to dinner at eight o'clock in a coat made from wool which had been on a sheep's back at five o'clock the same morning. After careful consideration John Coxeter said it could be done and the sporting baronet laid a wager of 1,000 guineas on the venture.

On June 25th Sir John sent his shepherd, Francis Druett, to Greenham Mills with two Southdown sheep. The sheep were shorn, the wool was washed, stubbed, roved, spun and woven. The cloth was scoured, fulled, tented, raised, sheared, dyed and dressed and ready by four o'clock for the tailor, a Mr James White of Newbury. The coat was cut out and nine men were ready, with needles threaded, to make it up. The work was finished by 6.20 pm and Sir John Throckmorton appeared wearing the coat to the delight of the 5,000 people who had assembled outside the mill. The two sheep, which had been killed and roasted whole, were distributed among the people together with 120 gallons of ale, thoughtfully provided by Mr Coxeter.

Sir John, accompanied by 40 friends, sat down to dinner at the George and Pelican Inn. The coat, a hunting type of the fashionable Wellington colour (a damson shade) is still in existence and is on display at Coughton Court, the principal seat of the Throckmorton family (now in the hands of the National Trust).

As a footnote, Mr Coxeter might not have so generously aided the peace celebrations (see below) had he realised the effects the ending of the

The Newbury Coat, worn by the grandson of John Coxeter, Mr John James Coxeter, c1900. (West Berkshire Museum)

Napoleonic wars would have on the cloth-making industry. The market for cloth slumped and in 1817 the family sold off all the machinery of which John Coxeter had been so proud.

Peace Celebrations

Mr Coxeter gained further local renown when he presented a plum pudding, 24 ft in length, to eight hundred poor people in Greenham as part of the celebrations with which Newbury greeted the signing of the Treaty of Peace on 3rd May 1814. A year later the victory at Waterloo called for more rejoicing. The Corporation, together with the Yeomanry and Volunteers, attended a service at the parish church. The very substantial collection was given to the fund which provided for the widows and orphans of those who had not returned from the campaign.

Trade in the 19th century

Improved road conditions and the increase in the use of the Kennet and Avon Canal brought about a renewal of prosperity in Newbury. Although the cloth trade never revived, the felt makers still worked in Whirleygog Lane (now called The Arcade), and other trades were introduced to augment the older industries of the town. Alongside the cloth mills, corn mills, maltings and breweries which had been part of the town's source of revenues for centuries, new industries began to appear. The town's gasworks opened at the Cheap Street end of King's Road in 1825 and by the end of the year the town was lit by gas. Increased demand, partly arising from its later use for cooking and heating, led to a new and larger gasworks being built in 1880 at the corner of King's Road and Boundary Road. Brick-making yards and iron foundries also provided employment for many. William Plenty had come to Newbury at the end of the 18th century and set himself up as an agricultural engineer and metal founder. This was a time of innovation in agricultural machinery and within a few years Plenty had invented a new design of plough. But he didn't stop at that and, in 1816, he invented an 'unsinkable' lifeboat which was launched at West Mills. When the forerunner of the RNLI placed fourteen lifeboats around the coast of Britain in 1824, eleven were made in

Greenham Lodge showing the high quality wood panelling and staircase by Samuel Elliott & Co, Newbury. (West Berkshire Museum)

Newbury. A little later in the century, Plenty's were making stationary steam engines, the type of engines used to drive machinery in factories, timber saw-mills and on farms. From these were developed steam engines to power coastal shipping. All of this work was done in the centre of the town, where the Kennet Centre now stands. The company only moved to their present premises, in Hambridge Road, in 1965. Another new business was Albert Steam Joinery Works (where Bayer is now). Samuel Elliott started the business around 1870, manufacturing high quality wood carving, moulding and joinery work (eg panelling and staircases), for fitting out churches, banks, country houses (including Greenham Lodge) and other large buildings. Ownership changed following Samuel Elliott's bankruptcy in 1895 and Elliott's Moulding and Joinery Company Ltd was formed; they will be referred to again in the next chapter.

Machine Riots

Terrible scenes occurred in the neighbourhood during the Machine Riots in November 1830. The farm labourers were demanding higher wages and less machinery, especially in regard to the new threshing machine, as this caused unemployment. They rioted, and supported by a mob of hooligans, marched on various farms, breaking up all farm machines, setting barns and ricks on fire and, in some cases, burning down the houses. A detachment of the Grenadier Guards was sent from London to help quell the riot and all the townsmen who could come mounted were told to assemble in the Market Place. They paraded at mid-day with the former Donnington Castle and Newbury Troop of Yeomanry. At Speenhamland they were joined by another company of horsemen which assembled at the George and Pelican. Trotting to Gravel Hill at Stockcross they were strengthened by more mounted men, led by Lord Craven. They moved off along the Bath road towards Kintbury, which was the centre of the disorder, with the Guards following in coaches. Another party under Colonel Dundas and Captain Houblon joined them at the Kintbury turning. The horsemen surrounded the village while the Guards and others searched the houses. The rioters were mostly found in the public houses, and many arrests were made. Inkpen, West and East Woodhay, and Highclere were then searched; and altogether about a hundred men were taken into custody. Only one Berkshire man was executed, but many were transported or sent to prison.

Newbury Union Workhouse

To alleviate the extreme hardship of the poor the Newbury Union Workhouse was built in 1835 at a cost of £5,000, but no one sought this refuge except as a last resort. Apart from the shame felt by people entering the workhouse, families were split as there was strict segregation of men, women and children. Able-bodied inmates had to do physical work and many were employed growing vegetables on the institution's land.

It remained a workhouse until well into the 20th century when, under new legislation, it became the responsibility of the Ministry of Health, and locally and nationally conditions began to improve for the under privileged. Much of the old 19th century building remains today, but many new additions transformed it into Sandleford Hospital with services for geriatric, maternity and physiotherapy patients. By the close of the 20th century some of these services had moved to other hospitals, largely due to a reorganisation of health services. At the beginning of the 21st century it seems likely that all of these premises will be demolished and the site sold, to offset the costs of the new hospital for the area which is to be built at Turnpike Road.

Queen Victoria's Marriage

The celebration of the Queen's marriage in 1840 took a practical form. A public subscription raised sufficient money to give every elderly person 1s 0d per head, every other adult, 8d and every child living in a family, 4d. This enabled 3,200 people to enjoy a good dinner in their own homes. It is to be hoped that the money was spent as intended!

Dinner parties were held at the Mansion House and in all the principal inns of the town.

The Railway

Its favourable position on the road network had built up Newbury's prosperity over the centuries and the canal had brought further advantages to the town. The advent of the railway was, therefore, watched with unease as it spelt disaster for both the canal companies and the coaching trade. The Great Western Railway completed its line between Bristol and London via Didcot and Swindon in 1841. From then on heavy goods that had previously travelled by canal between Bristol, Newbury and Reading and thence along the Thames to London could be carried by rail at half the cost and in hours rather than weeks, along a track that was not liable to freeze over in winter or dry up in summer. As the railway network quickly developed, the country was opened up to new goods; sometimes these replaced local products. For example Simmonds brewery at Reading was more economically able to sell its beer over a wide area, including Newbury, whilst Welsh roofing slates were soon distributed over the whole

Newbury Station c1905.

of Britain. This quickly led to the closure of the local clay tile industry as slates themselves were cheaper to use. Also, because they were lighter in weight, roof structures could be constructed less expensively. This contributed to the change of appearance of local building styles.

Likewise the railway transformed the pattern of long distance passenger travel. The stage coaches could not compete in terms of speed, cost, and not least comfort. As each new section of line opened up so travellers switched to the train. The coaches were required to cover an ever diminishing portion of the route. The last stage coach between Bristol and London ran in 1843. Newbury, lying halfway between the two, felt the loss of its passing trade keenly. Many famous coaching inns closed and the large number of people they employed were put out of work. Without the revenue from coaches at their tolls, the turnpike trusts, which maintained the roads, went bankrupt. Development and improvements in road surfacing were abandoned. The Bath Road lost its bustle and glamour and became once more a quiet country track, lying in peaceful neglect until the coming of the motor car at the end of the century.

The railway brought a new prosperity to the towns it linked. Reading, connected by rail to most parts of the country, grew quickly from a market town into a busy commercial and administrative centre. Newbury had at first been by-passed by this new artery of communication. However, in 1847, a branch line of the Great Western opened from Reading to Newbury and Hungerford. This was later extended to Westbury and ultimately to Penzance.

Later, the Didcot, Newbury and Southampton Railway Company was formed to provide the vital north-south rail link. The GWR agreed to operate the line when it was built. Work began in 1879. The Didcot to Newbury section opened in 1882, and Newbury to Winchester in 1885. The opening in April 1882 was marked by gigantic festivity in Newbury; the entire town was decked out in flags and flowers. The grand procession of dignitaries to the inaugural train included a detachment of the Royal Berkshire Yeomanry Cavalry, the band of the 93rd Sutherland Highlanders,

Northbrook Street; a watercolour painting of c1840. (West Berkshire Museum)

and Newbury's Fire Brigade with engine and four white horses.

Although not the principal cause of the rejoicing, these celebrations coincided with the final agreement by the GWR to improve facilities at Newbury Station. Before then there had simply been two very short platforms, with a shelter on the up-line only, described by one unhappy passenger as 'an undersized chicken coop'. Following the improvements of 1882, the station was further altered in 1900 and then completely rebuilt between 1908 and 1910 as part of the upgrading of the line which had now become the major rail link to the West of England. The result is the building that stands today together with the present line layout of two through tracks and two platform loops. Originally there were also three bays, but the two western ones have been removed and their sites used for car parking. A line was opened from Newbury to Lambourn in 1898. It was operated for seven years by the Lambourn Valley Railway Company before being taken over by the GWR.

During the first four decades of the last century the railways became steadily less profitable as competition grew from the new generation of motor vehicles and roads. Finally, after intensive use during the Second World War, it became obvious in the 1950s that some of the lines running through Newbury would have to close. Passenger traffic on the Didcot-Newbury-Winchester line ceased in the early 1960s and in 1966 the line closed completely. Passenger traffic on the Lambourn line stopped in 1960 but the section between Newbury and Welford Park earned a reprieve until 1973 because it serviced the American Air Force munitions depot at Welford. A three mile stretch of line connected the base and Welford Park Station. Finally, this section too closed after a dispute as to the cost of repairs to bridges along the track. A final nostalgic train for enthusiasts was run on 3rd November 1973. Newbury was then left as a main line station only, with good services to London and the West Country, and connections for the north and south of England through Reading.

Enclosures

Throughout the 19th century Newbury lost some of its common lands although it became apparent during the course of the inquiries that some had disappeared during the previous century – legally or illegally.

The East and West Fields were officially enclosed between 1846-1849 against considerable opposition. The City Recreation Ground was awarded by way of compensation.

The Wash suffered a similar fate in 1858 although it was pointed out at the public meeting held in 1855 that the common had been granted to the Mayor and Corporation by King Charles I in 1627 (as in fact had all of the common land through the Borough's purchase of the manor). Since that date it had been a favourite place for horse racing. Allotments for poor labourers, and a recreation ground on the edge of Enborne, were given as compensation in this case. Stroud Green has remained open land and The Marsh has been transformed into Victoria Park.

Northcroft held on to its grazing rights but with the passing of time few wanted to turn out hogs and cattle. Consequently there was little interest when a meeting was called in 1953 to end these rights. The vote was carried and it enabled the cricket pitch to be fenced off on what once had been fiercely contested common land.

The Newbury Weekly News

Throughout the century several attempts were made to start a local newspaper without success but in 1867 J. Walter Blacket and Thomas W. Turner were more fortunate. Their paper, the *Newbury Weekly News*, became well established and continues to this day to cover not only the news of Newbury but of surrounding areas too, while representatives in several villages send in items of interest. Property for sale or rent now comprises a separate section and a monthly business supplement and a bi-monthly leisure magazine, *Out and About*, are included with the main paper. A weekly free paper, *The Advertiser*, is delivered to a number of homes and since 1996 Thatcham has had its own free paper, *Thatcham News*.

Late Use of the Parish Stocks

News was made in Newbury in 1872 when it appears to have become the last place in the country to use the stocks as a form of punishment. For years they had lain discarded and dusty in the Town Hall but a certain Mark Tuck, a well known drunkard, was sentenced to four hours in the stocks for insobriety and for causing a disturbance in the parish church. As it was a very wet day the stocks were placed in the shelter of the Shambles and a policeman was on duty to ensure that the prisoner suffered no physical harm from the youths who gathered round to jeer him. On his release Mark Tuck lost no time in leaving the Market Place.

The New Cattle Market

No doubt the sale of sheep and cattle was originally in the Market Place, but by the early 19th century it took place in the yards of various town centre inns. It was all very inconvenient and it was with relief and celebration that the farmers and townspeople greeted the opening of the cattle market in 1873. It was situated in Market Street which had been widened to allow better access. On the morning of the 18th December

Newbury from the south, c1840; view sketched from a position just below Chandos Road. (West Berkshire Museum). See also page 183.

flags and evergreens were suspended near the two gateways. At eight o'clock precisely the Mayor, Joseph F. Hickman, pronounced the market opened for tolls, and the pens were quickly filled.

The church bells rang throughout the morning in anticipation of further formalities. At three o'clock the Mayor and Corporation, together with Lord Carnarvon, the County Members, the Magistrates, and other gentlemen, met at the Council Chamber and walked in procession to the new market. Lady Carnarvon preceded them in her carriage and awaited their arrival.

The unloading pen, suitably decorated, was used as a dais because of its elevated position. A crowd of two to three thousand had gathered but were soon brought to silence by the Town Crier as the dignitaries took up their positions.

Lord Carnarvon formally opened the market which was duly inspected before the procession reformed and returned to the Town Hall where a banquet for 240 guests had been prepared.

Extensions were made to the market in 1915 when the Mayor, F.D. Bazett, performed the opening ceremony on 30th September but the market closed in 1968 and was demolished to make way for the multi-storey car park which, in turn, was replaced by the present bus station.

The Town Hall

The first floor of the fine 18th century building in Mansion House Street (see page 62) was essentially a suite of assembly rooms where balls and other entertainments could take place. However, it seems that it was also used for some of the administration of the Borough's activities. These had increased following the Municipal Corporations Act of 1835 and the growth of public services during the Victorian era. In 1878 a new building opened facing the Market Place containing offices, a Council Chamber and, on the ground floor, the Magistrates Court. The clock tower completed the building in 1881. More space was soon needed and it was also felt that Mansion House Street needed to be widened, so the old Mansion House/ Town Hall was demolished and the extension to the municipal offices opened in 1910. This was about two thirds the depth of the former building.

Borough Extension

A substantial extension of the area of the Borough took place in 1878 when part of the parish of Speen (mainly in the north and east, including Donnington Square, Speenhamland and Woodspeen East – near the Robin Hood) and part of Greenham (west of Pile Hill and north of Stroud Green), were brought within its boundaries.

Throughout the country the population of towns had grown as rural labourers moved from the countryside to take advantage of the better opportunities which the towns were perceived to offer. Towards the end of the century, very wealthy people (who had often made their money in the factories and new types of businesses which had developed in the Victorian era) moved out of the towns and cities and built new homes in the countryside. The railway made it practicable for men whose business was in London to live well outside that city. Examples in this area are Lloyd H. Baxendale, a partner at Pickfords transport company, who bought the manor of Greenham in 1856 and built Greenham Lodge in 1875; E. Festus Kelly, proprietor of the indispensable commercial directories, had Hollington House built in 1904; and the eminent architect William Waterhouse, who designed the Natural History Museum in London, moved to Yattendon and built a new house in 1878. Many other less prominent people built large houses on the high and healthy common lands around Newbury.

Hospitals

The building of the Didcot/Newbury/Southampton railway line brought about a spate of accidents and a hospital was opened in Enborne Terrace c1880 to which the injured workmen could be taken.

In 1885 the Newbury Hospital was opened on the site of the present hospital in Andover Road. It had just twelve beds but was soon enlarged and during the First World War it was used by both civilian and military patients. After 1918 it was remodelled and enlarged at a cost of £37,000. Although major cases are now treated at the Reading and Oxford hospitals the local hospital is still of major importance to the townspeople with its friendly staff and welcome visits from the local doctors. In 2001 work is due to start on a new hospital for the area. This will be sited at the eastern end of Turnpike Road and will replace both Newbury and Sandleford Hospitals. Several million pounds of the cost will come from a bequest of land at Wash Water to Newbury Hospital Helpers League by Miss Rosemary Rook (see also page 83).

Golden Jubilee Celebrations

Another gala day dawned for Newbury on 21st June 1887 when Queen Victoria celebrated her Golden Jubilee. Residents were left in no doubt that the festivities had commenced when that relic of the Crimean War, a twenty four pounder Russian gun, was fired from the Marsh at 6 am. There was a thanksgiving service in the parish church where a stained glass window was unveiled by the Mayor, Mr Benjamin Smith. Another United Service took place at the Corn Exchange. Outside, in the Market Place, twenty three tables, laden with food, awaited the local children. Another salvo at 11 am started the mammoth procession; at one o'clock the children sat down to consume 1,500 lbs of meat, a ton of plum pudding, and 300 gallons of ginger beer and lemonade. The leftovers were distributed to those who had walked in from neighbouring villages. In addition, every street organised its own party. In the evening the town was illuminated and bonfires blazed from the surrounding hills.

Fair Dispute

The townspeople were not quite so united in 1893 when a dispute arose regarding the Michaelmas, or hiring, Fair. The origin of this fair is obscure. It was not granted by royal charter but by Statute or Ordinance of the Corporation as lords of the manor, so that dates it after 1627 and prior to 1752 when, owing to the alterations in the calendar, it was announced that 'the Market for Hiring Servants, which used to be held here on Thursday next after Michaelmas day, will this year be held on Thursday, the 12th day of October next, and will for the future be continued to be holden on Thursday next after the Old Michaelmas Day.'

It was this custom of hiring servants that caused the controversy. The Corporation considered that the custom, which was already on the decline,

East Newbury from the air, 1899. The photograph was taken from Rev J.M. Bacon's gas balloon which had just taken off from the new gasworks sited in King's Road. A crowd of upturned faces watches from Boundary Road, as a train passes underneath the bridge on the former line from Newbury to Didcot. (D Liddiard)

was degrading and outdated and should be abolished.

As at other hiring fairs, it had been the custom for men and women who wanted employment to line up at the fair with symbols of their trades.

92

A cowman would display some cowhair, a carter some whipcord and a shepherd a piece of wool, while the maids carried a mop and the cooks a spoon. Employers could take their pick, and it was understood that the employment would be for the coming year provided that there was satisfaction on both sides.

At first there was opposition to the abolition of an old custom, although some, particularly those who lived near the Market Place where the fair was held, thought the fair should be completely abolished. Eventually, after a ballot had been taken, it was decided to end the hiring of servants but to continue the fair for amusement only. It stayed in the Market Place and overflowed into the Wharf until the Second World War prevented it from being held. It was resumed in 1945 but caused so much disruption to the traffic that it was moved to Northcroft the following year.

The End of the Century

In 1895 work was commenced on a project which had been under discussion for 25 years – an efficient drainage system for the town. Walter Money described it as 'one of the most successful undertakings with which the governing body has been connected.' It was indeed of first importance if the epidemics which beset the town from time to time were to be eradicated, and the general health and comfort of the townspeople were to be improved.

Many prosperous traders still lived above their shops and had first hand knowledge of the plight of some of their neighbours who lived in the numerous alleyways and back streets of the town.

Town officials, caring tradespeople, church and chapel goers, all combined to try and improve the conditions of the poor. Clothing and coal clubs, and soup kitchens, were opened. Concerts and other entertainments were organised in an effort to keep adults out of the many public houses in the area, and children were encouraged to attend Sunday schools.

Education in general was improving and the new Grammar School was opened for 80 day boys and 20 boarders in Enborne Road.

A surge of loyalty on the occasion of the Queen's Diamond Jubilee in 1897 brought about another festive day when for a brief spell all troubles and hardships were forgotten. The borough presented the Queen with a congratulatory address and a representative committee of townsmen arranged the celebrations which concluded with a magnificent firework display, the ringing of bells, the beating of drums, and the singing of the National Anthem. An observer at Woodhay counted 53 bonfires blazing around the town.

It was indeed a memorable celebration to mark an era, and a century, which was drawing to a close.

------------CHAPTER SEVEN------------

The Twentieth Century

Introduction

In 1901, Newbury could still be seen as a market town, providing an outlet for the produce of local farms and a range of supplies and services for people living in the area. There were still many people living and working in the countryside. Even quite small farms still employed several men, looking after livestock and the land and there were rural industries, such as brick-making and wood turning. The country estates, often centred on the historic manor houses in many of the villages surrounding the town, employed, in total, large numbers of people as indoor or outdoor staff. For the day-to-day needs which country people could not provide or grow for themselves, most villages had small shops, often including a baker and a range of craftsmen, such as builders, joiner/undertakers, shoe repairers etc. However, it was to the town that people looked for more specialist services and a larger range of goods. In many instances these were provided by family-owned firms and profits made tended to be spent in the community. By the end of the century things were completely changed and almost everything was made or sold by national or international companies.

Even in 1901 the writing was on the wall. Plenty & Co and Elliott's Moulding and Joinery Company were referred to in the previous chapter. Both of these firms sold their products throughout southern England. Likewise, other specialist firms supplied their products to the Newbury area. There was also the beginning of the chains of grocery shops which developed into the supermarkets which dominate food retailing at the end of the century. Other national firms, such as chemists and booksellers, also had a foothold. Improved roads and the railway system had made this more economical than fifty years earlier. As mentioned, the railway had begun to bring changes in the 19th century and had resulted in the loss of the tile-making industry. In the 20th century the brick-making industry in this area also closed down in the face of competition from large-scale manufacturers. So far as the consumer was concerned, a much greater range of products was available, but local varieties were lost. Already, in the 19th century, as Britain's empire had developed, a range of tropical and sub-tropical products had become available, at prices which could be afforded by growing numbers of people.

Following the 1914-18 war, the experiences of men who had served in the forces had made fewer willing to work as servants to the wealthy. In any case, people continued the exodus (which had started in the previous century) from the countryside to the towns, where they thought there were better opportunities. As business, and indeed life, became more complex, increasing numbers of people were employed in office-based work – administrators, accountants, solicitors, designers, and people involved in marketing, advertising and sales. Soon after the end of the 1939-45 war, the Atomic Weapons Research Establishment was started on the site of the wartime airfield at Aldermaston. At another former airfield, at Harwell, the Atomic Energy Research Establishment was opened. These brought many scientists and technicians to the area and housing for some of them was built at the southern side of Newbury. Many people from the area also obtained employment there. Opportunities for training in technical work opened up for people who, for example, might otherwise have been employed in unskilled work. The number of scientifically trained people seems to have aided the development of the electronics industry in and around Newbury in the last quarter of the century.

Indirectly this may, in turn, have contributed to Vodafone being based in the town. Racal originally set it up here in 1983 before anyone knew how rapidly the demand for their services would grow. Following organic growth and after merging with similar firms, Vodafone has become one of the largest companies in Europe. In 1981 the international pharmaceutical company, Bayer, based the headquarters of its British company in Newbury. The position of the town, in the centre of southern England and at the intersection of several roads, allied with changes in transport patterns late in the century, led to the area developing as a major distribution point. Both Newbury and Thatcham have growing commercial areas and redistribution depots. The main factors were the building of the M4 in 1971, the development in the 1970s of Portsmouth as a cross-channel commercial port and the international container port at Southampton. The traffic generated by these two latter developments led to the improvement of the A34 as a link between those ports and the Midlands – as part of a European route from Spain to Scotland.

All of the employment opportunities from these new businesses have led to Newbury becoming one of the most prosperous towns in the country, with a very low level of unemployment. Conversely, this has a downside, as house prices are so high that potential first-time buyers are unable to afford them and roads are crowded as people have to live further from their work places. All this inevitably leads to demands for new housing areas. This then causes friction with those people already established in the area, who see such development as a threat to their local environment and the value of their homes.

So it is against this background of changes throughout the century that the following sections need to be read.

Town Expansion and Housing

House-building had started along the roads built on the sites of the West Fields and East Fields (based around Craven Road and Queens Road) in the last quarter of the 19th century and continued in the 20th. These were built as single or semi-detached houses or short terraces. Larger houses with more spacious gardens were built along Andover Road, at Speen, Pyle Hill and elsewhere. At the other end of the scale, many working class families were still living in tiny houses in the many courts and yards behind the main streets of the town. A survey in 1917 described the conditions of these, some of which were appalling. Many received very little daylight – rear rooms sometimes being without windows; most shared a wash-house with only a small open area for drying; and often two or more families shared one outside water tap and outside closet. However it was not until the 1960s that the tenants of the last of these were finally rehoused. In 1920 the first council houses were built, in St George's Avenue, and by 1973 the Borough owned 2,384. Immediately after the First World War, the aim nationally was to build 'Homes fit for Heroes'. There

The Clock Tower and Broadway in 1940.

was a clear need locally to provide modern houses for rent by the poorer members of the community and to rehouse those displaced from the slummy courts and yards of the town. In April 1934 the boundaries of the Borough were again extended, to recognise the true extent of the town. The largest area added was taken from Cold Ash and Thatcham. This provided the land for much new housing built from the 1950s to 1970s, both by the council and private developers, in the Kiln Road, Turnpike Road and Lower Way areas. A smaller section was taken from Enborne between Andover Road and Enborne Street. This formed part of the site for the 1970s' 'Bovis' estate of private houses.

Houses in the Valley Road and Wendan Road areas were built by the government in the 1950s and 60s to house Aldermaston and Harwell employees. Whilst private building had always taken place, usually of a small number of houses, the 1960s saw the arrival of large estates of private houses. This seems to have been due to a greater number of young people wishing to buy their own homes, rather than renting them which had been the more usual practice of the previous generation. Mortgages were also available to people in a broader range of employment. Older people also bought homes on the new estates, rather than continuing to pay rent. By the 1980s as land became scarcer, house-building began to take advantage of smaller areas of land and many house-owners with large gardens sold off part of their plots for the building of one or two new houses. Another change which began in the 1960s arose from the growth in car ownership. This made it easier for people to live in more characterful houses with rural surroundings in the villages, whilst working in the town. By the end of the century, as a result of growing demand, villages have been expanded with new housing – though the increase in the values of rural houses has often put them outside the purchasing power of long-standing village families.

It was around 1972 that John Norgate, a Newbury entrepreneur, set up a company named Trencherwood. Initially this was concerned with residential property development, but later added commercial premises to its interests. Like any developer the company was criticised, but, living locally, Mr Norgate did give financial support to many local projects. Trencherwood quickly became profitable and converted to a public company, many local people purchasing shares. The company's developments stretched from the south coast up to the Midlands and

The River Kennet, with St Nicolas' church in the background, 1955.

South Wales and they also built up an extensive land-bank, ie purchased land, or options on land, with future development potential. Sadly for investors, the bursting of the property bubble late in 1988 resulted in a dramatic fall in land values, and share prices followed. This, and the early death of John Norgate in 1995, led to the take-over of Trencherwood by David Wilson Homes in 1996.

Newbury has had an unusually large number of almshouses for several centuries, many due to the bequests of cloth makers. Several of these charities have now been amalgamated, but they continue to provide cottages and sometimes other benefits. During the second half of the 20th century, local authorities provided a number of blocks of 'old people's flats', usually with a warden in residence. In the last decades there has been growth in the number of commercially built retirement homes. These have allowed people to move from larger properties to ones of a more easily manageable size, whilst retaining their independence. The communities thus formed also provide security in that neighbours would soon be aware if others were ill or needed help. In Newbury several of these are close to the town centre enabling their residents to shop and take part in the town's activities.

Town Government

For most of the 20th century, Newbury Borough Council was responsible for running the town services, with Berkshire County Council providing education, social services, the police and fire services etc. The Borough had also had responsibility for education until the 1944 Education Act transferred this to the county. The reorganisation of local government which took placed on 1st April 1974 resulted in the extinction of borough, rural district and urban district councils. Much larger local authorities replaced them and Newbury District Council took on duties for the western half of Berkshire. The County Council retained the services it had previously provided and took over some others, including libraries. From the same date a new police authority, Thames Valley Police, was formed covering Buckinghamshire and Oxfordshire in addition to Berkshire. New companies, such as Thames Water, were formed throughout the country to take over the former civic functions of water supply and sewage treatment and disposal. Although the Borough no longer existed, the Government accepted the desire of old towns such as Newbury to continue their traditions and allowed the setting up of charter trustees. However, these bodies had no real power and could not charge rates; they could only ask district councils to provide a modest sum for their expenses. The Newbury Charter Trustees were made up of the district councillors for the wards which had formerly covered the area of the Borough and were allowed to call their chairman Mayor. Some people, especially those who had lived under the historic Borough Council, were frustrated by the lack of a council which had the interest of the town as its aim. After all, Thatcham and Hungerford, previously of lower status than Newbury, had town councils (in legal terms the same as parish councils) which could raise rates, provide services and give a voice to their communities. However, authority was eventually obtained and Newbury Town Council was formed in April 1997. The new local council was able to take over provision of some services, such as the market and allotments in the town, and anticipates taking on other property and services from the district council in 2001 or 2002. Newbury Town Council was able to appoint its own Town Clerk and other support staff, including a town crier. It also appointed a town manager to liaise with shopping and other commercial interests and to ensure that, as a town, Newbury remained competitive and attractive. The chairman of the council is Mayor of Newbury, continuing the centuries-old tradition.

All of the other 1974 arrangements continued until a further reorganisation on 1st April 1998 resulted in the abolition of Berkshire County Council and the formation of six new unitary authorities to provide all the services (except police) in the county area. The unitary authority covering the area previously managed by Newbury District Council is West Berkshire Council. The Berkshire Fire Service and County Record Office are operated as joint services by all six unitary authorities.

Transport

The sections on previous centuries have referred to the changes in long-distance transport from pack ponies, wagons and stage coaches on the roads via barges on the canal to railway wagons. However, one local firm, J.J. Davies & Sons, china merchants in Northbrook Street, had their own narrow boat which they used on the canal network, to collect supplies from the Derbyshire and Staffordshire potteries, probably into the 20th century. This boat was kept at Wellington Wharf, near to The White House pub. Grain, whiting from Kintbury and other goods were carried on the Kennet and Avon Canal and in the late 1940s salt for Newbury Laundry was brought from Cheshire using inland waterways. Otherwise, by 1900 there was little competition for the railway. Obviously, the final stage of delivery had to be by road. The GWR employed their own delivery vehicles, or owners could collect their goods from the railway goods yard or station, or employ a local carrier to do so. One or two businesses had their own railway sidings; Plenty & Co could load steam boilers and engines directly from their boiler works in King's Road and the gasworks received coal (and dispatched coke) directly from railway wagons. Whilst horse-drawn vehicles would have been used at the beginning of the century, lorries became more common as motor technology improved. This was given a boost by the sale of surplus military vehicles at the end of the 1914-18 war – and again after World War II. At the beginning of the century, Newbury was served by three railway lines, but two of these were closed in the 1960s. This made the increased use of road transport inevitable and by the close of the century long-distance road transport became the norm.

A growing proportion of the population has recently begun to question the value of this as the mass protests against the building of the Newbury by-pass (opened 1998) proved. Whilst many local people felt that almost any price was worth paying to remove heavy traffic from the town, others considered that the destruction of beautiful countryside and the threat of infill to the west of Newbury placed too little value on the environment. The demonstrations against building the by-pass were not the first against such projects, but they were reported internationally and seemed to represent a new peak in the nation's concern for the environment.

There had been calls for many years for Newbury to be by-passed which had resulted in earlier improvements to the local trunk roads. The construction of Western Avenue in the late 1950s had removed A4 traffic from part of London Road and the Broadway and the opening of the M4 to the north of the town in 1971 took long distance east-west traffic away

1996. Security officials attempt to remove by-pass protestors from their tree houses. (Reproduced by kind permission of Newbury Weekly News)

from the town altogether. The first section of the A34 (now A339) to be improved was in 1966, from St John's Road to London Road, forming the Newbury relief road. This meant the rebuilding of the bridge over the railway, truncation of Cheap Street and division of King's Road as well as a new crossing of the River Kennet. A new section from London Road/ Western Avenue towards the M4 followed in 1977 and led to the construction of the first version of the Robin Hood roundabout. Finally, a new length from Monks Lane to join the relief road was completed in 1979. Nationally, the increase in road traffic seemed to keep pace with new road building: the new route might have reduced heavy traffic using the historic town centre, but did little to alleviate the delays that 'Newbury' represented to users of the trunk road! The completion of the by-pass enabled most of Northbrook Street to be pedestrianised (except for buses) during the daytime and the popularity of this led to the northern length of Bartholomew Street and Mansion House Street also being pedestrianised. The layout and paving of the Market Place had already been enhanced and these improvements together brought a new, more pleasant atmosphere to the town centre. From the late 1990s several new cafes in the Market Place, some with tables outside, and pubs with access to the river front added to the town's attractiveness.

Local deliveries by tradesmen and suppliers also changed from horse to motor powered transport, particularly after 1945. Whilst in the earlier part of the century carriers operated a regular service from and to outlying districts from a base at one of Newbury's many inns, later they collected from their customers' premises. As they became mechanised, some of them developed their service into one which primarily carried passengers, a local bus service, though they continued to carry packages and parcels into the 1950s. In 1932 several of these amalgamated to form Newbury and District Motor Services Ltd, operating a fleet of buses. At about the same time they extended their operations to run excursions to attractions or to the coast. The company was later sold, but continued to use Newbury Wharf as the main bus station. In the early 1970s a new bus station was built at the corner of Bartholomew and Market Streets, as part of the Kennet Centre development. About a decade later the buses moved back to the Wharf area whilst the Kennet Centre was expanded and a new car park erected. The present bus station in Market Street was then created on the site of a former multi-storey car park. Twenty years earlier this had been built on the site of the cattle market. At the end of the century we find the District Council trying to encourage more use of public transport, bicycles and car-sharing, in an attempt to reduce road congestion and the effects of pollution by motor vehicles. A number of cycle routes were laid out, generally to make it safer for pupils to cycle to school, and reduce the number of cars involved in the morning and afternoon school runs.

Shops and Shopping

Until the middle of the century there were shops which one wouldn't now expect to find in the town centre. There were several bicycle and motor dealers, all of whom would carry out repairs. In the days before gramophones or CD players there was much music-making in the homes of the better off. The premises of the musical instrument dealer Alphonse Cary in Northbrook Street supplied their needs. Even today violins and pianos bearing his name appear on the market. J.J. Davies & Sons Ltd were china and glass dealers, founded in 1847 where MacDonalds now stands. Such was their reputation that customers came very long distances. The shop was also unusual, as in a section which had been formed from the former carriage entrance, a large grape vine grew! Shopping was a much slower process than now as there was no self-service. Even groceries were sold 'loose' and had to be poured, cut or weighed and everything was individually wrapped. Chairs were usually provided for lady customers to sit on whilst they were being served. Wealthy customers would not shop regularly for foodstuffs, but when it came, for example, to jewellery, clocks or china, some would arrive in their carriage (or later their car) at the door of the premises and expect the proprietor to go out to serve them! Today certain types of business are segregated, but until well into the century, manufacturing took place immediately behind the street frontages. Plenty's engineering works was between Cheap Street and Bartholomew Street, Elliott's furniture works just behind the Methodist church in Northbrook Street and breweries and maltings in several locations.

Apart from the fact that by 2000 all large shops, except Camp Hopson, belong to national companies, another major change is the great number of premises now found in the shopping centre which are not selling goods ie estate agents, building societies, travel agents and banks.

Camp Hopson was formed in 1921 by the amalgamation of two established family-owned firms and has steadily increased the size of its business. In 1998 it opened a large modern building adjacent to the River Kennet to house its furniture and furnishings departments and so release space in its main shop. Of the national chains, the Singer Sewing Machine Company and Freeman Hardy and Willis's shoe shop opened around 1900. The first food suppliers were David Greig, soon after the first war, and Macfisheries: both closed near the end of the century. But the first of the modern High Street Stores to come to Newbury was Woolworths in the 1920s (when they sold nothing that cost more than sixpence ($2\frac{1}{2}$p)). Marks & Spencer opened in 1935. W.H. Smith opened a shop on Newbury Bridge at the turn of the century. As well as selling books and pictures they ran a printing works and lending library. Boots, the chemists, arrived in 1936, next door to their rival Timothy Whites, who had been open since the beginning of the century. In the 1980s, after they had become one company, the shops were rebuilt as one new large unit.

A big change took place in the early 1970s when a large area of old buildings between Cheap Street and Bartholomew Street was demolished and the first phase of the Kennet Centre was built. A decade later this was expanded to the north and west and the originally open square, roofed over. Whilst Sainsbury's was an important focus of the centre from its opening, in 1994 it moved to new premises to the east of the relief road. A little before this, in January 1991, Tesco moved from the west side of Northbrook Street to new premises off Pinchington Lane, but retained a town-centre presence next to Marks & Spencer. These moves took place at a time when, nationally, out-of town shopping centres were being built. The idea was that land costs and rates were lower and that ample car parking could be provided for customers. Most of the town's car dealers began to move to the Motor Park at Pinchington Lane in 1996 and the following year Newbury Retail Park opened in the same area. There had previously been some moves away from the town centre – in the 1980s and 1990s – when a number of retailers and motor dealers had opened larger premises in London Road. The traditional markets on Thursdays and Saturdays continue to operate in the Market Place, though even here the nature of the food and goods sold has changed and some vendors travel long distances.

Employment and Manufacturing

During the first half of the century much employment in Newbury was related to farming and rural activities. In or near to the town there were watermills at West Mills, Town Mills (Hovis owned both of these from 1921 to 1957), Greenham Mills and Ham Mills, on the River Kennet; Bagnor, Donnington and Shaw mills on the Lambourn and Washwater Mill on the Enborne. Adjacent to Greenham Mills was Holland Brothers' steam-powered mill. All of these ground wheat or other grain, including animal feed. There were several maltings in the town, which first sprouted, then roasted, barley as the raw material for brewing beer. Whilst some of this would have been used in the town's three breweries (there were ten in the 19th century), more would have been sold in London or elsewhere. Much of the locally-grown grain would have been sold at the weekly Corn Market, held in the Corn Exchange. Between the wars this was an important market in southern England. Although the corn market continued until the 1980s, towards the end it was on a very small scale, and only a handful of farmers, seed and grain merchants and dealers in other agricultural products met on a Thursday morning. The local grain and seed merchants who had premises in the town (notably Dolton's and Midwinter's) had all closed or moved out by the 1980s. The cattle market, too, closed in June 1969, having had two weekly sales until the early 1960s. Newbury's abattoir, off Faraday Road, also closed about this time. These closures reflected national changes in the way that cattle and other livestock were sold. Similarly, supermarkets led to the closure of greengrocers and their sale of locally-grown vegetables and produce, apart from small amounts in the twice-weekly markets. Supermarkets also led to the demise of local butchers, fishmongers and grocers. However, at the beginning of the 21st century there is growing concern about the quality of food and there is a network for the distribution of locally-grown organic vegetables. Newbury held its first 'Farmer's Market' in 2001, where producers sell directly to the customer.

From soon after the first war, Day, Shergold and Herbert held a weekly auction of eggs, poultry, butter, vegetables, flowers and other local produce, in their sale rooms in Wharf Street (now occupied by The Hogshead pub). Buyers came from London and other large cities and in the 1920s, for example, more than 30,000 eggs were sold each Thursday.

By the 1970s sales were falling and the auction finally closed in 1987. Dreweatt, Watson and Barton, who ran the Cattle Market auctions, and A.W. Neate & Sons were both land agents and managed farms as well as being surveyors and estate agents. They merged in 1987 to form Dreweatt-Neate and have offices across central southern England. During the second half of the century, Dreweatt's developed their fine art auctions and in 1980 restored Donnington Priory as a base from where they now operate a business which enjoys a national reputation. The Priory also houses the headquarters of their agricultural department.

Although Newbury is surrounded by farmland, at the end of the century unlike the beginning, there was little visible evidence in the town of businesses providing for the needs of farmers, nor any obvious link between the town and their produce.

Elliott's of Newbury have been mentioned when referring to the 19th century. In the 20th their business concentrated on making a range of furniture, particularly bedroom and dining suites. They were chosen to exhibit in the Festival of Britain exhibition on the South Bank, London, in 1951. Their normal production was interrupted by both world wars. In the first war they made over 200,000 ammunition cases, with unskilled labour. In the second war they made substantial sections of aircraft, including Mosquitos, Spitfires, Airspeed Oxfords and a high proportion of the large troop-carrying gliders for the D-Day landings. At the end of the war they were employed in making complete rooms for the pre-fabricated homes installed throughout the country. In 1945 they were not at first allowed to return to furniture manufacture, so, through the interest of the managing director, Horace Buckingham, they made a series of sports gliders including the *Olympia*. These were successful in competitions and some are still in use today. They also designed and made a light aircraft, the *Newbury EON*, but this did not go into production due to the state of the British economy. Manufacture of the gliders continued after furniture manufacture resumed in 1948, but ceased soon after Mr Buckingham's death in 1965. For a long time the company was Newbury's largest employer. There were six hundred on the payroll during the war years and over five hundred people in 1965, though this rapidly decreased and was down to one hundred and fifty when they ceased trading on the Albert Works site in 1974. Bayer and the Northcroft estate now occupy the site.

Craftsmen working on an 'Olympia' glider at Elliott's in the 1950s. (West Berkshire Museum)

Engineering is a business frequently overlooked when thinking about the employment opportunities in Newbury, yet significant manufacturing still takes place in and around the town. There is in fact a long tradition of metal working in Newbury. As archaeological evidence shows it was taking place in the town centre from the 12th to at least the 16th centuries. Plenty & Co have already been referred to, but they have not made engines for many years and now specialised in the manufacture of filters, mixers and pumps, mainly for the oil and gas industries.

Opperman Mastergear Ltd's products are sold around the world. In Newbury they manufacture industrial gear drives for conveyor systems, container handling, mining, pumping and mixing, and actuators for the controlled opening and closing of valves for the water, oil, chemical and other processing industries. Their business began in Newbury when Opperman Gears moved to Hambridge Road, from London, in 1940. In

1987 they merged with Mastergear who had been founded in Newbury in 1962 and then the combined company was sold in 1991 to the Regal Beloit Corporation of Wisconsin, USA.

UK Solenoid has been established on the corner of London Road and the relief road since their factory was built in 1971. They developed from the Chilton Aircraft company, based around Hungerford, but a year or so after moving to Newbury the Austrian firm of Kraus and Naimer bought out the British directors. There are several other firms manufacturing products ranging from domestic water-softeners to refrigeration equipment and a variety of constructions produced by metal engineering companies. They are mostly based in the industrial estates in the London Road/Faraday Road and Bone Lane/Hambridge Road areas.

New Greenham Park is an interesting development. Following the armed forces vacating Greenham Common the whole area was bought by Greenham Common Trust (set up by Sir Peter Michael) for £7 million. The Trust then sold the airfield to Newbury District Council for a symbolic £1, retaining the areas used for aircraft hangars and the facilities and accommodation for American troops. The retained section was then transformed by the Trust into an industrial/commercial area, New Greenham Park. A large proportion (£100,000 in 2001) of the rents generated are being used to aid local community projects. Restoration of the commonland to its natural state as lowland heath, which is now a rare habitat, is also being financed. Part of the restoration led to the aircraft runways and taxiways being dug up and the concrete crushed. A considerable amount of this hardcore was used in the construction of the Newbury by-pass.

Reference has been made earlier to the effects made on the Newbury area by the opening of the Aldermaston and Harwell atomic research establishments and the development of high technology industries in the Thames Valley/M4 corridor. Big changes took place in the town during the last three decades of the 20th century as the electronics industry developed. The first to make an impact was Quantel, which started life as part of (Sir) Peter Michael's Micro Consultants at West Mills in 1969. It became a separate company in 1973 and after other ownership changes regained independence following a management buy-out in 2000. The firm developed the conversion of images to a digital state and then led the world in the manipulation of television images, image storing and film editing. Others were Norsk Data, the Norwegian computer manufacturer and supplier, who came to Newbury in 1980. They purchased and restored the 18th century Benham House, west of Speen, and also built two adjacent blocks of offices. The company moved into the new complex in 1985. Subsequently they sold the property, though still occupy offices there. The business was reformed as Nextra in 2001, following a merger with two other companies. Kerridge Computer Company specialise in computer software, particularly for the motor industry and vehicle fleet operators. Having been founded as a bicycle shop in Alton, Hampshire in 1907, they came to Newbury in 1979, three years after their computer operation began. They moved to premises in Northcroft Lane in 1982/3 and in 2001 transferred all operations to their Hungerford base. Merant, who are now based at The Lawn, Speen Lane, came to West Street, Newbury as an office of the international company Micro Focus, in 1983. They, too, are software specialists, initially specialising in the mainframe language, Cobol, but then also writing for desktop computers.

Another change in the employment possibilities of Newbury came with the opening of corporate headquarters. In 1981, Bayer plc, the international pharmaceutical and chemical company, moved the headquarters of their UK and Ireland company to new offices on the site of the Elliott's factory (see above). Their aim in moving from Richmond was to obtain a better quality of life, including the office environment and commuting experience of employees. They needed somewhere with good communications – railway, motorways and closeness to Heathrow, as most of their managers need to travel a great deal. Their staff are all managerial, administrators, or involved with sales or marketing. They brought a range of qualifications to the town as many are highly qualified professionals, including chemists and doctors of medicine. They were not the first offices dealing with substantial sections of a national company's business. Kleinwort Benson, the merchant bankers, hold this honour, having opened offices dealing with share registration and other aspects of their business administration, at The Lawn, Old Bath Road, in 1958. The company's headquarters was in the City of London and they were still developing when they moved from Burghclere to Speen, initially employing around twenty staff. But the mid 1970s they had grown and already extended the Georgian building and by the end of that decade had added a large octagonal extension, facing the A4. They were one of Newbury's largest employers until the late 1980s with over three hundred staff. The office closed in 1991, most staff being transferred to their head office in Fenchurch Street. In 1995 the company was taken over by Dresdner Bank and are now part of Dresdner Kleinwort Wasserstein.

All of these are overshadowed by Vodafone, which currently employs 3,500 staff. Yet only sixteen years ago its service began as a minor subsidiary of the electronics firm, Racal. At the time most mobile phones were referred to as car-phones. They were heavy and needed fixed charging apparatus in a vehicle. Vodafone became independent in 1991. As well as car-phones the company also sold electronic pagers, which by a pattern of 'bleeps' let owners know they were needed and by whom. Soon the possibility of transmitting brief text messages to a new model of pager made them even more useful, but at about the same time relatively lightweight fully portable phones came onto the market and quite rapidly the demand for phones soared. By 2001 it is said that virtually every school child has a mobile phone. Text messaging was launched exclusively by Vodafone at the end of 1994, but more recently has become a craze as messages are sent and received via mobile phones. The number of text messages grew from 2.5 million in April 1998 to 222 million in December 2000. There were 11 million sent on New Year's Day 2001, the largest number ever on one day.

Vodafone soon outgrew its original offices and took on more buildings until in 2001 they occupied more than sixty different buildings spread around the Newbury area. However, in the same year the construction of their new World Headquarters was underway, to the north of Love Lane. The choice of this site was not without controversy as it was agricultural land and outside the area scheduled for development by the district council. After long consideration, and taking into account the threat by the company to move from Newbury, permission to build was given by the council. At the turn of the millennium Vodafone merged with AirTouch in the USA and Mannesman in Germany and since 1999 has been in the top ten European companies. Vodafone and other mobile phone operators have paid large sums to governments for the new 3G licences (transmitting licences for 'third generation' phones). Vodafone won the auction for the main British licence at a cost of £5.96 billion, as well as paying large sums to other European governments, a total investment of

The new Headquarters building of Vodafone Group plc, in construction during the summer of 2001. (Author)

£13.2 billion. As a giant company, its business is an interesting modern concept as it does not manufacture anything. It is an archetypal service company, providing mobile communications, processed by computers and transmitted through a network of masts and antennas.

In the mid-1980s and partly because of the Government's view that Britain's economic future lay with service industries, rather than manufacturing, the profile of tourism was raised. Growing numbers of people were beginning to take weekend breaks and Newbury, being in the centre of attractive countryside and within easy reach of established tourist venues was ideal. However, there was a shortage of accommodation in Newbury itself. Therefore, the district council encouraged the building of hotels and the use of private homes for bed and breakfast accommodation. Within the next few years several new hotels were built.

Newbury's Tourist Information Centre was moved to the museum building and upgraded in 1984. The new site was particularly appropriate as 'Heritage' was seen as Britain's main attraction for overseas holidaymakers. Newbury District Council also joined the *Beautiful*

113

Berkshire marketing campaign which was successful in bringing the delights of the area to a wide audience and substantially increasing visitors.

A development which improved communication about the area was the opening in 1992 of Meridian Broadcasting's newsroom and studio, with a staff of sixty, in Hambridge Lane. More news and features on West Berkshire are now shown on television. The parent company was sold to Granada at the end of 2000. Local radio, based in Reading, has been in existence since the 1970s and is currently represented by the commercial station 2-Ten FM and BBC Radio Berkshire. New community radio regulations led to the opening of Newbury's own station, Kick FM, in May 2000. But the longest-standing of the area's media is the *Newbury Weekly News*, founded in Northbrook Street in 1867. It will publish its 7,000th continuous edition on 12th September 2002. In 1952, a Central Office of Information film *The Local Newspaper* used the *Newbury Weekly News* as an example of the role of a provincial paper. As well as the mechanics of producing a newspaper, it showed many local activities and the work of the paper in reporting them. The company had changed from hot-metal to offset lithography in 1974, but completely modernised its editorial and printing operations when moving to new premises in Faraday Road in January 1982. A number of other newspapers are now published on its presses, as well as its own supplements. The current circulation of the *NWN* is between 27,000 and 28,000 copies each week. The paper is also the major backer of Kick FM. During the latter part of the century there were other free newspapers and magazines; currently there is the *Newbury and Thatcham Chronicle* and *Berkshire Life*. Publications about the locality have grown in number in the past twenty-five years. The publishers of this book, Countryside Books, have produced several titles (as well as a great number of others relating to the whole country), but others have been produced by individuals or societies. During the year 2000 many parish histories were produced to celebrate the Millennium. This growth has been made easier by the wide use of sophisticated home computer programmes, as well as new printing techniques.

The 20th century saw Newbury change from a typical market town to being a thriving modern business community. Unemployment rates for West Berkshire in May 2001 were the eighth lowest in the country, with 0.6% of the working population claiming unemployment benefits; in Newbury itself unemployment was even lower.

Leisure Activities and The Arts

Newbury Bowling Club claims to have been founded in 1598 and therefore to be the country's second oldest. At the beginning of the century the club had its green at Speenhamland, but in 1934 moved to its present site in Victoria Park. The new green and pavilion were built as part of the Newbury Work Creation Scheme (using unemployed labour during the depression) which improved the park's facilities and created Park Way. The pavilion had to be rebuilt following an arson attack in 1985. Cricket, rugby and soccer were played at a number of sites. Newbury Football Club's pitch was displaced eastwards to its present site as a result of the building of the relief road and development of Faraday Road industrial estate. During the century the borough and district councils have provided a number of other pitches for hire, including those at Victoria Park, Northcroft, Stroud Green and Wash Common. The largest facility has been provided at Henwick Worthy Field, between Newbury and Thatcham, where there are all-weather and floodlit pitches. This was opened in 1996, following the land being provided by Trencherwood as 'Planning Gain' for the community, in return for planning permission for house-building at Dunston Park.

Newbury Rugby Football Club (founded in 1928) also benefited when it was realised that their pitch off Pinchington Lane had development value. In partnership with Trencherwood, the builders of Newbury Retail Park, they were provided with a new clubhouse and pitches at the western end of Monks Lane in 1996. The club now has facilities suitable for international matches. All ages from seven plus are encouraged to play the game and a women's rugby team has been formed since moving to the new ground.

Golf has a long history in the area, as when Crookham Golf Club opened in 1873 it was only the seventh in England and first inland eighteen-hole course. Newbury District Golf Club opened in 1923 and in 1946 formally merged with Crookham as the latter's course had been lost through the building of Greenham Common airfield. In fact Newbury District's course had been reduced to seven holes during the war, partly due to an aircraft runway but also as they had to give up an area for sheep grazing! Crookham members had been invited to use the course as guests. For many years Newbury and Crookham Golf Club was the only club in the

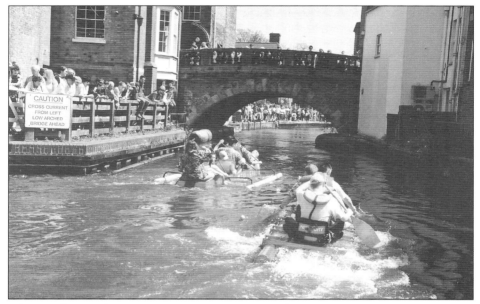

The Crafty Craft Race. Competitors near the finish in 2000. (Reproduced by kind permission of Newbury Weekly News)

immediate area, but growing interest in the game in the 1980s led to the creation of new ones, two at Donnington and others at Stockcross and Newbury Racecourse. There is also a driving range at Newbury Racecourse, planning permission for a nine-hole course at Pinchington Lane and six other courses within ten miles of Newbury.

Newbury Cricket and Hockey Club is based at Northcroft. This field also became the home of the town's swimming pool. Towards the end of the 19th century this had simply been formed from a stretch of the branch of the River Kennet which then flowed across Northcroft and Goldwell Parks. In 1937 it was completely modernised and a water-treatment plant installed, to form the existing outdoor pool. It was further improved and a paddling pool added in 1963, but in 1980 a new leisure centre was opened which included indoor pools and squash courts. Later a large sports hall and other facilities were erected. There was considerable growth in provision for leisure in the last two decades of the century and a number of private health and fitness clubs opened. An indoor bowling club also opened at Greenham, with financial assistance from the council, and a commercial ten-pin bowling rink was built in Lower Way.

The Waterside Youth and Community Centre was originally built as a youth centre in 1964 but now offers a wider range of activities. These still include drama and canoeing and a range of ball games but a climbing wall and parent-toddler and young parent groups have, for example, been added. The Devizes to Westminster Canoe Race passes through Newbury and the participants take a break at the centre. This race takes place each Spring, except that it was cancelled due to the foot and mouth epidemic in 2001 and curtailed in 2000 due to dangerous flood conditions on the Thames. The Crafty Craft Race is held each May when teams propel by muscle-power a variety of individually made craft from Hungerford (Kintbury for juniors) to Newbury. There is a great atmosphere of fun throughout the route and various entertainments in the Victoria Park and Newbury Wharf area where it ends. Organised by Newbury Round Table,

The Boxing Day meet of the Vine and Craven Hunt, 1989. (Reproduced by kind permission of Newbury Weekly News)

Newbury Races. Copper King *wins the first race of the inaugural meeting on 26th September 1905.*

the event raises funds for local charities. Newbury Carnival also ends at Victoria Park, but towards the end of the century had not received the support of forty years earlier. Fishing has been an activity of the area for centuries, Newbury was once well-known for its trout and crayfish. There is now limited free fishing in the town and many coarse fishermen belong to clubs which pay for the right to use the canal or gravel pits near Thatcham. River fishing, especially upstream from Newbury, is mainly fly-fishing. Trout fishing is limited to conserve stocks and rights are correspondingly expensive to rent. Fox-hunting was popular at the beginning of the century and the Craven and Old South Berkshire Hunts met regularly in the area. The Vine and Craven Hunt is now the one operating in this area. Traditionally the hunt met in Newbury's Market Place each Boxing Day and still did so at the end of the century. However, by then, there was much opposition to the sport, many believing it to be a cruel and elitist pastime. Even in the third quarter of the century there were large numbers of hunt followers who would support and observe the hunt from various vantage points. Although the number of these supporters may have decreased, a strong and vociferous following for hunting remains.

Always the Favourite. Queen Elizabeth The Queen Mother at Newbury Racecourse, Hennessy Gold Cup Day, 1996. (Reproduced by kind permission of Newbury Weekly News)

Newbury Racecourse was opened in 1905, although there had been race meetings at Wash Common earlier in the previous century, before the common was enclosed. The racecourse was the idea of John Porter, a leading trainer based at Kingsclere. He is reputed to have enlisted the help of King Edward VII after the Stewards of the Jockey Club turned down his initial proposal. The opening meeting in September 1905 attracted a remarkable field of runners and 15,000 spectators, which assured the racecourse's success. Racing was interrupted by both wars and the course's role in these will be described later on. Improvements were made to the course and stands in the twenty years between the wars, but it was April 1949 before racing could resume after the Second World War, at what is one of the country's finest racecourses. Substantial improvements were made by major new buildings erected in 1992 and 2000, replacing the old stands and incorporating exhibition rooms, restaurants and other facilities. Reference has already been made to Newbury Golf Centre at the course and a health club also has a centre there. All of the non-racing activities indicate how racecourses have to diversify now to help recoup the large investment needed to keep their facilities up to date. Racing, of course, continues to be the main activity and races are held throughout the year, both flat and national hunt. In recent years a number of evening meetings have been held. The main race meeting is that in December, focused on The Hennessy Gold Cup. HM Queen Elizabeth The Queen Mother is a fairly frequent visitor to the course and HM The Queen and other members of the royal family also attend meetings.

Newbury & District Agricultural Society have held an annual show since 1909. In 1985 they purchased land at Prior's Court, adjacent to junction 13 of the M4 where they have developed a permanent showground, with roadways and entrance gates etc. The showground is already used for a small number of displays and exhibitions each year. The Newbury and Royal County of Berkshire Show is held during a weekend in September. As well as many livestock and other farming competitions, and marquees with competitive exhibitions of crafts, food, flowers and plants, there are several arena displays. The show currently attracts around seventy thousand visitors and the displays usually end (weather permitting) with a massed take-off of hot-air balloons. This has developed from the interest of local farmer (now retired) David Liddiard and an acknowledgement by balloonists of the co-operation they receive

*The Newbury and Royal County of Berkshire Show, September 2000.
(Reproduced by kind permission of Newbury Weekly News)*

from the farming community when landing their craft. Back in 1972 Mr Liddiard had been approached by balloonists wishing to use land he farmed at Marsh Benham for balloon ascents. For several years Marsh Benham was a well-known centre for ballooning and local people became accustomed to seeing these colourful forms floating in the sky above Newbury. An annual balloon meet – the Icicle Meet – was held during the first weekend in January from 1973 until 1992 when, following Mr Liddiard giving up his tenancy, the Icicle Meet moved to his son's farm in the Savernake Forest area. Ballooning, including passenger flights, still takes place in West Berkshire, but fewer balloons are seen over Newbury. During the 1970s and 80s there were aerial displays of another kind, when every two years there was a major international air display at Greenham Common Airfield. These had to cease with the upgrading of the base security when it was being prepared for cruise missiles.

Some of Newbury's many sports clubs have been mentioned earlier in this section, but additionally there are a large number of clubs and associations which cater for almost every other interest, from art to wargames. As with all towns there are clubs for business and professional men, such as Rotary, Round Table and Lions, and Freemason's Lodges were established in the 19th century. The 20th century also saw the foundation of clubs for educated and professional women, Soroptomists, Ladies Circle, Senior Wives and Inner Wheel, the female side of Rotary. The three main political parties also have their associations. Two long-established organisations with specific interests are Newbury District Field Club, found in 1870 to study the archaeology, history and natural history of the area, and Newbury Symphony Orchestra, which started as Newbury Amateur Orchestral Union in 1879, and is the second oldest amateur orchestra in the country. The Field Club has a programme of lectures and visits (though its range of interests now extend further than the immediate locality) and also publishes a journal recording the results of research into this area. Two others which have historic and environmental aspects of Newbury as their interests, and were founded in the second half of the century, are the Newbury Society and Newbury branch of the Kennet and Avon Canal Trust. The National Trust, National Association of Decorative and Fine Art Societies, Berkshire, Buckinghamshire and Oxfordshire Wildlife Trust and the Council for the Protection of Rural England, all have local branches. There are, of course, many others as referred to at the beginning of this paragraph. The heyday for clubs was probably a little before, and in the two decades after, the Second World War. By the end of the century several were finding difficulty in persuading their members to take on the responsibilities of organising their activities; Newbury's two Townswomen's Guilds closed on that account, despite enjoying relatively large memberships. Finding new, younger, members who will involve themselves is increasingly difficult. In some ways society is becoming more passive and perhaps feels it can gain sufficient entertainment and information from television, the internet and books, rather than join with others of similar interests to learn together.

However, there are groups and individuals who do create things. Members of Newbury Operatic Society, Newbury Choral Society and other choirs sing music together and give concerts, as does Newbury Symphony Orchestra. Members of these and other musical groups came together in the 1920s to give performances as Newbury Musical Festival; its name was changed in 1979 to Newbury Festival of Choirs. Their performances have been conducted by such eminent musicians as Sir Henry Wood, Ralph Vaughan-Williams, Adrian Boult and Sir Malcolm Sargeant. For a period from 1940 into the 1970s Newbury String Players, which was formed from a mix of professional and very able amateur musicians, performed regularly over a wide area. They were formed and led by the composer Gerald Finzi, who lived at Ashmansworth. Following his death in 1956, his son Christopher took over the Players. More recently Southern Sinfonia, an orchestra of professional musicians, has been based in the area. In 2001 the renowned musician Sir Roger Norrington agreed to become their patron. The orchestra has its origins in a small group of musicians led by Miranda Wilson at Boxford in 1980.

Several painters, printmakers, potters, textile artists, sculptors, furniture and musical instrument makers and other crafts people work in the area. Each year, in May, there is the opportunity to see the work of many of these through the 'Open Studios' scheme. As the name implies, some of them also demonstrate their abilities. Newbury Art Group exhibits its members' work and also holds classes to help novice members. Throughout the 1980s and 1990s the Arts Workshop, housed in the former Temperance Hall in Northcroft Lane, showed regular exhibitions of craft and art work. They also hosted plays, poetry readings, recitals and held a range of courses and activities involving the creative and performing arts. Each year there were also art exhibitions at the Museum. For different reasons both of these venues ceased art exhibitions in 1998/9, the Arts Workshop closing down. At about the same time, Greenham Common Trust made buildings available for arts use and New Greenham Arts was formed. They have extensive exhibition space and an auditorium for performances, together with several workshop areas for hire by artists. It was announced in July 2001 that the Corn Exchange (see below) was to take on the management of the facility.

At Bagnor, just outside the town, is the Watermill Theatre. This was formed from a mill building and since 1968 has staged a programme of professionally acted plays throughout the year. Patrons travel long distances to enjoy the performances given in such delightful surroundings. Since 1993, Newbury has had an excellent performance venue in the re-modelled Corn Exchange. The Corn Exchange was built in 1862, partly to improve the conditions for selling grain, but from the outset also to provide an indoor venue for the town. The building was used for a great variety of activities: roller skating, church fairs, exhibitions and civic events. During the second war many popular dances were held there – especially after the Americans were based at Greenham. The famous band-leader Glenn Miller gave one of his last performances there before his plane went missing over the English Channel in 1944. The interior underwent a remodelling in the 1930s and later a false ceiling was installed and the stage area improved.

It remained popular for ballroom dances and dinners, but in the 1960s and 70s several pop concerts were held there, some with acts who were, or became, big stars. Wrestling bouts were another type of entertainment that drew capacity audiences during the same period. Such 'choreographed' fights formed popular television programmes at that time. Several of the larger music and dramatic societies in the town also hired the hall for performances. But there were always periods of time when no activity or performance took place, entertainment depended on some organisation or individual hiring the venue. Then, calamity; in 1988 it was discovered that there were structural defects and that the 1950s interior fittings were considered a fire risk. The building was closed. As the town had lost its other venue, the Plaza Theatre (now Dreweatt-Neate's car park), shortly before, entertainment in Newbury faced problems. Some organisations were able to stage performances in school and church halls, but these all had limitations. The cost of restoration was at first seen as prohibitive, and all but the facade of the building was threatened with demolition. There were objections to this locally and from national organisations and the hall simply stood empty. Then, in May 1991, there was a change in the political balance of the district council. The decision was made to restore and improve the building. The roof was removed, the building stripped to its basic structure and a steel girder frame built inside to support the roof and reduce the strain on the walls. The laminated wooden roof trusses were identified by English Heritage as an early use of this form of structure. They were preserved in situ and are again exposed to view. The interior was remodelled to provide ramped seating, which can be folded away, an improved stage area and additional floors at the front of the building to improve the entrance and provide bars and a meeting/ rehearsal room. Easy access for physically disabled people was also ensured and a lift installed. The building was extended at the rear to provide management offices and changing rooms and other facilities for

The Regal Cinema in Bartholomew Street, c1950. (West Berkshire Museum)

performers. Since its completion it has had a permanent professional staff and there has been a varied and almost nightly programme of events which has met with approval and audience support. In 2000, West Berkshire District Council agreed that management of the facility should be delegated to an independent trust, which had financial advantages to both the council and the venue.

Reference has been made to the Arts Workshop. In 1978, when fund raising to convert the building was nearing completion, it was decided to hold a short series of music concerts. This was arranged under the patronage of the then Lady Porchester (now the Countess of Carnarvon). Its success led to the proposal that a regular annual festival should be held, and so the Newbury Spring Festival was born. This now provides an annual fortnight of mainly musical events held in and around Newbury for two weeks each May. Many of the world's great musicians and orchestras have taken part. Most major concerts are held in St Nicolas' church or the Corn Exchange, but other events are held at village churches and some of the great houses in the area. Lady Carnarvon remains President of the Festival and HRH The Duchess of Kent was its Patron for twenty-one years from 1979. The Duchess has been a regular visitor to the Festival and HM The Queen has also made a number of private visits.

Despite a national resurgence in film-going, Newbury ended the century without a cinema. Apart from the Corn Exchange showing an up-to-date film most weeks, Newbury people have to travel to Reading or Basingstoke. The Newbury Cinema was opened in 1910, at the southern end of Cheap Street, by local entrepreneur Jimmy Tufnail. A month later another was opened, Newbury Picture Palace, immediately south of the Methodist church in Northbrook Street. This building still stands and the slightly overhanging upper floor which housed the projection equipment can still be seen. Grander buildings followed in the 1920s producing the Regal Cinema in Bartholomew Street (closed 1962) and the Central (later Carlton) in Cheap Street (destroyed by fire in 1950), with the Forum in Parkway in 1939. This last operated under several names, including ABC and Cannon, finally as a Robins Cinema when it too closed in November 1998. Throughout the country many cinemas closed or converted to bingo halls in the late 1950s and 1960s, following a steep fall in audiences as more homes acquired television sets.

Food and Eating Out

A different way of spending leisure time also grew towards the end of the century as the increasing number of restaurants, pubs and bars show. Coffee shops, too, were a phenomenon of the 1990s as several national and international chains opened branches in Newbury. Two decades earlier burger chains had spread from the USA, followed by shops selling take-away roast chicken, then kebabs and pizza restaurants, all offering a quick service. A little later services offering home delivery for pizzas and other foods for immediate consumption began. These are obviously national trends, but form part of the evidence of our towns losing their individuality, also people's expectations (brought about by marketing and advertising) of finding such products available in their locality. In the final decades of the century, shops and supermarkets offered a growing range, and improving quality, of ready prepared chilled or frozen meals. All this also linked with more women continuing to work after marriage and having less time for home cooking, whereas earlier in the century many would have started families soon after marriage and expected to spend the rest of their lives looking after their homes. Buying meals was not a new idea in itself; inns, restaurants and cafes had long provided for the traveller and wealthy person. The main difference was that in the earlier period most facilities would have been opened by individuals or families. Now they are provided by large firms directly, or as franchises where someone invests capital or pays rent or a 'royalty', but follows set recipes and has the ingredients supplied. Fish and chip shops had opened early in the century, and ice-cream parlours and milk bars in the 1930s. In the late 1950s there were coffee bars selling *cappuccino* in wide, shallow cups and in the same era Chinese restaurants became more widespread. A little later Indian restaurants, eventually offering regional cooking styles, and Italian restaurants opened in almost every town.

Examples of all of these were present in Newbury. They all showed Britain's growing interest in other cultures and lessening of its insularity and a greater awareness of the flavour of foods. Until the 1970s, Newbury still retained 'traditional' English cafes, which had served travellers and visitors to this market town through the century. One very well-known from the 1930s to 1970s was the Tudor Cafe, on Newbury Bridge, which had its own bakery and restaurant where a number of local organisations met, and was run by the Hole family. Others were Spring's Cafe, London Road, The Bandarlog Cafe in Northbrook Street, The Corner House at the Wharf and The Welcome Cafe in Cheap Street. Of course many new ones have opened and Camp Hopson have had the Penthouse Restaurant in their main building for many years and opened the Upper Deck in their new building overlooking the Kennet. Nor are coffee bars a new thing. In the 18th century (and possibly late 17th) there was at least one coffee house in Newbury; the building still stands at the southern end of the Broadway, bearing the name 'The Kings Coffee House'. At the beginning of the century the Temperance Movement (in Newbury this began in the 1870s) was in full swing, persuading people from the 'evils of strong drink'. This was at a time when too many poorly paid working men were spending most of their wages on beer, at the expense of food and clothing for their families. In 1879 the movement opened a temperance hotel and coffee house in Mansion House Street and, four years later, the Fountain Coffee House in The City.

127

The Elderly

The area around Argyle Road, Derby Road and Newtown Road has been known as The City since the early years of the 19th century; previously it was called Bartholomew's – from the medieval hospital at its core. Although there are almshouses and sheltered accommodation in other areas of the town, a particular concentration has built up in the part of Newbury in and near The City. St Bartholomew's Almshouses are the oldest established and Raymonds' followed at some date prior to 1676. A building which may originally have been a medieval farm building was adapted to provide the accommodation. The arms of the Brewers Company, carved in stone and dated 1670, are mounted on the exterior of the building. They relate to Philip Jemmet, a brewer who founded the almshouses. His son-in-law and daughter, Sir Jonathan and Lady Raymond, further endowed the almshouses and from then their surname is attached to them.

New almshouses were built for the charity in the 1790s in Newtown Road, with a further group (Upper Raymonds') parallel to Derby Road in 1826. The original Raymonds' building was used as the Church Almshouses after they were vacated by Raymonds' almspeople, but in 1928/9 they were purchased and remodelled by Dr Essex Wynter. He gave the building an additional floor and converted it into homes for nurses retired from the Middlesex Hospital in London. He had purchased the building immediately north as his own home and re-named it Bartholomew Manor. In the same period he bought the cottages on the corner of Pound Street and also constructed a new building, modelled on Raymonds', and completed in 1937. All of this was to provide further homes for the Middlesex nurses. As Dr Essex Wynter's estate proved to be insufficient to maintain the property, Lord Astor provided a substantial sum to improve the homes. After the Second World War, and as a result of other bequests, several bungalows to the south and west of the original homes were added to the group. The church almspeople ceased to use the Argyle Road property in 1879 when new almshouses were built in Newtown Road (south of St John's Road) for the combined Church and Childs charities. Off Pound Street and immediately behind the nurses' home, a Mr Ravenshear built a block of four flats for elderly people. This was demolished around 1990 and The Argyles Nursing Home has been erected on its site.

In the 1960s Newbury Borough Council wished to improve facilities for the elderly and built new premises, partly on the site of the St Bartholomew's Almshouses which had been destroyed by bombing in 1943. This was called The Fair Close Day Centre and also incorporates blocks of flats to the side and rear. It was opened by HM Queen Elizabeth The Queen Mother in 1967. In addition to providing a social centre, the building also houses the kitchens where food is prepared for the Meals on Wheels service, as well as hot lunches for users of the centre. To the rear of these premises is Link Road where there are several blocks of flats suitable for elderly people. A little further east are more flats in Catherine Road and Ashridge Court. Other facilities for the elderly, sick or disabled members of the community are the Handybus Service which provides transport for people attending groups such as the Stroke Club and hospital clinics. A volunteer system provided by private car owners is available to take people to hospital appointments in Newbury, Reading or Basingstoke. There is also the Red Cross and several clubs for people who suffer from specific illnesses or disabilities, who run day or half-day activities and are also able to give help and advice to patients and their carers.

Education

Newbury has the normal range of schools providing education for pupils from five to eighteen years old. For the first half of the 20th century, the schools for infant and junior age children were all close to the centre of the town and, with one exception, in Victorian buildings. At the century's close, all were in modern buildings and most in the 20th century suburbs where people now live. For even younger children, the town has a nursery school, started in a building in the centre of Victoria Park in 1942. This was to help mothers to be employed in war-work. The need for it continued after the war and in 1989 it was replaced with a new school at the northern edge of the park with accommodation for 78 children (although as most are part-time twice as many as this can attend). Near the end of the century other nurseries and creches opened as more women wished to continue their careers after childbirth.

At the other end of the age range are the facilities of Newbury College. This was set up by Berkshire County Council in 1948 as Newbury

St Bartholomew's Grammar School; an aerial photograph taken in 1938.

Institute of Further Education, at Ormonde House which now houses the administrative unit of the college. In 1999/2000 it had 663 full-time and 11,343 part-time students. The College offers students a large range of courses in academic, vocational and leisure learning subjects, some of which are available at over fifty venues throughout West Berkshire. The College's site is cramped and, as it has grown in stages, comprises many buildings. In 2001 work started on a new forty-acre campus south of Monks Lane; due for completion in August 2002. The college became independent of the local authority in 1993 and has raised the £16 million cost of the new buildings through the Government-promoted Private Finance Initiative. Currently it is the only completely new college being built in the country.

Two of the three comprehensive schools have been referred to (see pages 29 St Bartholomew's, 41 Trinity), the third is Park House School at Wash Common (see also page 40). This began as a boys secondary school in 1947, as a replacement for the school bombed in 1943, which for a time had been housed at Shaw House. It became a mixed comprehensive school in 1975 and its facilities were gradually expanded. In 1996 it opened a sixth form, prior to which its pupils had to go on to St Bartholomew's. Until its amalgamation with Shaw House School in September 1999, there was a further secondary school, Turnpike School, to the south of Gaywood Drive. There was much local opposition to its closure, but as the number of pupils at both Turnpike and Shaw House was too small to enable a full range of facilities and subjects to be offered, the district council decided they must merge. Pupils from the east of its catchment area transferred to Kennet School, Thatcham. Apart from St Bartholomew's and the Girls High School, there was no secondary school in Newbury until 1934 when the Council Modern Boys and Girls School opened. This followed the raising of the school leaving age and an instruction from the Board of Education that all senior boys and girls were to be segregated in one building. The new school was formed from a section of the Boys and Girls Council schools opened by the borough in 1909. After the bombing of 1943, it was this secondary school which was transferred to Shaw House. There is a further school which has special links with Newbury. This is Christ's Hospital, at Horsham, West Sussex, a public school (see page 62). There are also several private schools in the area, including St Gabriel's School, for girls, at the edge of the town in historic Sandleford Priory (see page 22). Two national schools for pupils with disabilities are also nearby. The Mary Hare Grammar School, for deaf children, is at Arlington Manor, Snelsmore (with a junior school at Greenham Lodge from the 1990s) and a pioneering school for autistic pupils is housed at Prior's Court, Chieveley. The Castle School at Donnington is a council-run facility for children with special educational needs.

Education does not finish with colleges and universities and many people develop their interests and knowledge less formally. Newbury Library is a source for many. In 1905/6 the building in Cheap Street was erected with the help of a grant from the Carnegie Trust. The library was built partly on the site of the 18th century workhouse – made redundant with the building of the new one at Sandleford – and Town Gaol. A beam from the old building is incorporated into the gable of the library. This was extended by the Borough Council in 1968 and its entrance moved to Carnegie Road. As part of the local government reorganisation of 1974, control of the library service was transferred to Berkshire County Council. In the 1990s it was accepted that a new library was urgently needed and a site was found alongside the River Kennet. Building work was barely

Newbury Library, opened in July 2000. (Author)

under way when the County Council was abolished (April 1998) and the new West Berkshire Council completed it. The new library is much more spacious and light than the former one, and it opened to general acclaim on 31st July 2000. Apart from books, and other material which can be borrowed, the new library is well equipped with computers and film readers providing other sources of information in addition to more traditional reference works.

Another channel of information is West Berkshire Museum. The basic task of a museum is to collect the objects which represent our culture and its development, and also specimens from the natural world within which human activity takes place. In many instances the objects collected, along with the information related to their discovery, provide the only source of knowledge about an activity or period of human progress. Study by specialists results in books, articles and displays, which make an understanding of human activity more accessible to all. The museum's display galleries show a selection of objects from the collections, almost all of which are related to the area. A number of temporary exhibitions each year add to these more permanent displays. A great deal of the work of the museum's staff goes on 'behind the scenes' and information on the collections and locality can be made available by appointment. Newbury Borough Museum opened in December 1904 in the Cloth Hall, and its first collections included those built up by Newbury Literary and Scientific Institution from its inception in 1843. An extension between the earlier building and the Granary opened in 1934. Major restoration of the Granary was completed in 1978, and two years later the museum (from 1974 Newbury District Museum) was extended into it. This enabled substantial improvements to be made to its layout and range of exhibits. The entrance was moved to the Wharf at this time and the Tourist Information Centre combined with the museum shop. At the same time that West Berkshire Council came into being in April 1998, the museum's name was again changed, but its important local collections remain safeguarded for future generations.

More structured forms of further education are offered by evening and weekend courses provided by Newbury College, universities, or the WEA. In the 1980s a branch of the University of the Third Age (U3A) opened in Newbury. This comprises people who have usually reached retirement, working together in groups studying specific subjects and encouraging and helping each other's researches.

Churches

The 19th century saw a great increase in churchgoing and church and chapel building. Some of the latter arose from the formation of separate congregations of Nonconformists. During the 20th century, particularly the second half, this was reversed with numbers of churchgoers falling and buildings being demolished or put to other uses. Some Nonconformist churches, such as the Wesleyan and Primitive Methodists, amalgamated, whilst the United Reformed Church was formed from the Congregational and local Presbyterian Church in 1972. The third Congregational church built in Cromwell Place was completed in 1822 and extended fifty years later, but demolished 1958. The new church on the site was opened in 1961. The Baptist church in Northbrook Street was demolished in the mid-1930s and replaced with a church and associated buildings off the southern end of Cheap Street. In Bartholomew Street, the large Methodist church opposite Market Street was badly damaged by a gale during the 1940s and pulled down. The Presbyterian (later Unitarian) meeting house, built beside the Kennet in 1697, had not been used since the 1940s and was demolished in 1960. The Waterside Youth Centre is built on its site. Other smaller chapel buildings have also been demolished or used for secular purposes.

So far as the Church of England is concerned, St Mary's church, London Road was demolished in 1976, as were the mission churches in Boundary Road and Salcombe Road at the end of the century. On the other hand, the mission church of St Luke's, Wash Common was replaced with St George's in 1933, although the nave of the church was not completed until 1965. A new parish of St George the Martyr was formed in 1963 from part of St John's parish. The original church, which since 1933 had been used as a meeting room, was converted to a private theatre by the New Era Players when a new church hall was built in 1973. This, in turn, has recently been replaced. St John's church was destroyed by enemy bombing in 1943 and a replacement built after the war. The foundation stone of this was laid by

St John's church, completed 1957.

HRH Princess Margaret in 1955 and the completed church was dedicated in June 1957. These two church buildings will be referred to again in the architecture section of this book.

The Roman Catholics, too, have built new churches. Firstly St Joseph's in 1928 replaced the much smaller building of 1864 which still stands beside it. The bricks for the new church were made at Hermitage. The growing population of Newbury led to the formation of a new parish to the south of the town in 1965, dedicated to St Francis de Sales. Their new church was created from an ancient barn at Warren Lodge, Wash Common and was first used on Christmas Eve 1970. Many other religious organisations draw their members from the town and surrounding area and either have their own meeting halls or use school or other community premises.

Several churches were able to benefit from the value of land they owned. In 1964, St George's was able to sell surplus land at Wash Common for the building of Falkland Primary School, the proceeds enabling them to complete the church building and new vicarage. Twenty years later the Methodist church in Northbrook Street sold the former Wesleyan school and meeting room behind the church and received new meeting rooms in return. At about the same time St Nicolas' church demolished the old parish room and verger's house and built a new hall, other meeting rooms and a church office on a disused section of the graveyard. They also built an office block for letting on the site of the former buildings, the rents from which financed the redevelopment.

Public Services

Newbury's Police Station was at Pelican Lane, Speenhamland until the new Divisional Police Headquarters was built off Mill Lane in 1965. At the time policing was provided by the Berkshire force. In 1974 Thames Valley Police was formed by combining the Berkshire, Buckinghamshire and Oxfordshire county forces with the Oxford City and Reading Borough forces, creating one of the country's leading police forces. At the same time that the police station was built the courthouse was erected adjoining it. Prior to this the court had been situated on the ground floor of the Town Hall. From 1965, the new building provided court rooms and staff for the

Borough Quarter Sessions, the Borough and County Magistrates Courts, Juvenile Court and Coroner's Court. The justice system was changed soon after and for most of the final third of the century the court building provided the facilities for the West Berkshire Magistrates and Coroner's Courts. Tax Commissioners, Rating and Valuation panels, other similar bodies and the probation service also used the building. The Magistrates Clerk and other court staff moved from Newbury to Reading in 1997, although cases continue to be held in the Newbury courts. At the end of July 2001, it was announced that the West Berkshire Coroner for the previous forty-two years, Charles Hoile, was to retire. It was suggested that the post be combined with that of the Reading Coroner and cases heard there. Serious criminal cases are held at Reading. For centuries these courts were called Assizes, but in the early 1970s became the Crown Court. Civil cases are held at the County Court. For some time the Newbury Court operated from and heard cases in rooms above the National Westminster Bank, Market Place, but since about 1990 it has been wholly based in buildings in King's Road West. The County Court also operates the Small Claims Court.

Newbury Volunteer Fire Brigade was founded in 1878 to fight fires in the town. Inevitably they were also called to fires in the villages around Newbury. Until the middle of the 20th century they were based at Newbury Wharf, at first with horse-drawn steam-powered fire engines, but later with motorised vehicles. They were efficiently organised and held practices each week. This stood them in good stead both in fighting real fires and winning prizes at annual fire brigade competitions. Members were all employed in the town, but stopped whatever they were doing and ran or cycled to the Wharf when the alarm was sounded. In 1941, the National Fire Service was formed, based on existing brigades, and the volunteer service came to an end. Extra members were drafted into the new service, to man the additional fire pumps. Berkshire and Reading Fire Service was created in 1948 and whilst the core of the Newbury crew was full-time, two thirds were still part-time members. A new Fire and Ambulance Station was built in Hawthorn Road, adjoining the Robin Hood roundabout in the late 1950s. The ambulance service was transferred from local authority to Health Service control in April 1974. Around 1990, the fire brigade's important role in rescuing people from road accidents as well as other situations resulted in the renaming of the service as the Royal Berkshire Fire & Rescue Service.

Newbury's second gasworks had opened in 1880 at the junction of King's Road and Boundary Road. It was much larger than its predecessor and had direct access to the railway for coal supplies. It became redundant in the 1960s when natural 'north sea gas' became available through a nationwide system of pipelines. The present gasholder in Hambridge Road was erected to form the local reservoir. Electricity was soon to be introduced from generating stations in most sizeable towns – the National Grid, supplied from giant power stations, did not come until the middle of the century. Newbury's first public supply, in 1904, was provided by the Urban Electricity Supply Co from Greenham Mills. Here the first generators were powered by a water turbine, sunk beneath the floor of the mill building. Later this was supplemented by gas engines and diesel engines driving generating sets. Some, if not all, of these were made at Plenty & Co.

Mains water had been available in the town from 1875, when a borehole was sunk at Moor Lane, west of Northcroft and a reservoir with a capacity of 110,000 gallons built near Bath Road at Speen. Even so the immediate district around Newbury was not supplied until 1925. A water tower was built between Battery End and Falkland Road in the 1920s or 30s, to provide sufficient water pressure to the new properties at the south side of the town. Forty years later this was replaced with one holding 250,000 gallons, more than three times the capacity of the first. This remains in use and is a landmark on the high ground of Wash Common. As demand increased extra supplies had to be obtained and new boreholes were drilled at Cold Ash in 1931, with a pumping station in Fisher's Lane, and later west of Enborne Row. A new reservoir was built to the west of Wash Common in 1989, supplied from the new Enborne Row borehole and linked to the water tower. The reservoir at Cold Ash was also enlarged in the late 1990s.

Weather Extremes

At the beginning of the 21st century there is world-wide concern about the effects of global warming. Every time there is a spell of weather outside of the norm, then the finger is pointed at this modern phenomenon. Whilst not wishing to play down the very real and urgent concerns, it is as well to remember that there have always been unusual

Storm damage in Oxford Road, Donnington, January 1993. (Newbury Weekly News)

weather conditions! Gales, severe frosts and prolonged rainfall have been recorded for many occasions in the past (see pages 59 & 70). Further serious floods occurred in 1814, 1871, 1883 and 1894. In the 20th century improved drainage and control of the river greatly reduced flooding, though again in December 2000 some property, mainly in the Northcroft Lane area, was affected. There was a blizzard throughout England on 17th and 18th January 1881. Trains were stuck in drifts everywhere, almost a hundred barges were sunk at the mouth of the Thames and the pier at Woolwich was swept away by ice. In the Newbury area snow was blown in drifts reaching the top of hedges and the roads and lanes were completely blocked. At Cold Ash, a carter trying to get his wagon home died of exposure almost at his own door.

The most extreme weather of the 20th century includes the following: In 1908, there were several heavy snowfalls late in the season. On 4th March many telephone lines were brought down, emphasizing the importance of this new form of communication to subscribers. Although the snow soon melted, March was bitterly cold with gales and torrential rain. Then, on Saturday 25th April came a blizzard which lasted sixteen hours, causing the market to close early and tradesmen to abandon their deliveries. A wind of up to thirty five knots was measured and the heavy fall of snow was blown into drifts which made the roads almost impassable. The following day milkmen and bakers made their deliveries on horseback as their carts became snowbound. There was also heavy snow which lay for weeks during the winter of 1947. In 1959 sub zero temperatures lasted without break until March. In 1981 there was a late, heavy snowfall. By coincidence this also was on Saturday 25th April! The temperature dropped from 6°C during the day to freezing during the late afternoon and evening, then about six inches of snow fell and the wind speed reached twenty five knots. Trees were in full spring leaf and many were brought down, or great branches broken off, by the weight of snow. Many roads were closed and on the downland south of Newbury people were trapped overnight in their cars. Power and telephone lines were brought down and the Southern Electricity Board reported that the supply was cut off to nine thousand homes in an area of seven hundred square miles. They called out two hundred men in place of the forty-five normally employed in the area. The following day the snow melted, leaving the countryside littered with fallen trees and branches.

Newbury was on the fringe of the Great Gale of 1987, but on 25th January 1990 gales hit the town in full fury. The town centre was closed as slates and tiles were ripped from roofs and fallen trees blocked roads. There was extensive damage to property. Thousands were left without power or communications as the poles carrying electricity and telephone cables were brought down. It took days for supplies to be restored and the emergency services worked around the clock. Power and telephone engineers were brought from unaffected parts of the country to help with the work. There were lesser gales during the 2000/2001 winter which also brought down trees and power lines. The same winter and spring were excessively wet, the highest rainfall on record being experienced.

Visits by the Monarch

Perhaps this section might start with a visit by proxy – the statue of Queen Victoria. The Queen died in January 1901 and two and a half years later a statue to the 'Great and Good Queen' was unveiled by Mrs Reeve, daughter of the donor, 'Lord' George Sanger. Sanger was one of the great circus proprietors and showmen of the Victorian era and had been born in Newbury. He had requested that the statue stood on the site of his father's market stall. The figure of the Queen stood on a tall pedestal which in turn stood on a high four-armed plinth. Each arm of the plinth was guarded by a seated lion. In the niche between the front pair of arms stood a female figure representing Fame. The whole imposing edifice had been made from terracotta clay by Doulton's of Lambeth. The Queen's stay in the Market Place lasted only thirty years, for in 1933 the statue was dismantled and partly re-erected in Greenham Park. The plinth was reduced in height and area but with the four lions and 'Fame'. When Greenham Park was reduced by the new relief road, the statue was again dismantled and eventually re-sited in Victoria Park. This time it had lost part of its pedestal, the remainder of the plinth and two lions. It had also lost its original grandeur. 'Fame' remained in Greenham Park, though at some stage her raised arm holding a laurel wreath has been broken off. Somehow the two missing lions have found their way to Beale Park, Lower Basildon. Two other fragments survive, the Borough motto and badge are built into the external wall of the museum and the bronze plaque describing the gift is in the museum's collections.

Newbury Racecourse has regularly been visited by royalty, especially King Edward VII, HM Queen Elizabeth The Queen Mother and also HM Queen Elizabeth II. However, these are private visits, as are HM The Queen's visits to the Spring Festival. The Queen Mother also officially opened Fair Close Day Centre in 1967. HM Queen Elizabeth II has made two public visits to Newbury, the first on 26th May 1972. This was the occasion of St Bartholomew's Grammar School celebrating its Quincentenary and she visited the school to see various activities and exhibitions, including a model of the Berkshire Downs illustrating its geology and wildlife. Prior to this she had been driven from the Racecourse Station to the Market Place where she was greeted by the Mayor of Newbury and talked with townspeople in a way which would have seemed impossible a few generations earlier. On 25th October 1996, Her Majesty again helped Newbury celebrate an anniversary. This time it was the four hundredth anniversary of the granting to the Borough of its charter. After being met by the Lord Lieutenant (Mr Philip Wroughton) and being welcomed by the Mayor of Newbury (Cllr Gary Poulson), the Queen first visited the Council Chamber of the Town Hall. Here, the Charter

Royal Visitor. The Queen visited the town in October 1996 and is seen here talking to Mr Donald Willis, Chief Executive, Newbury Weekly News Group. (Reproduced by kind permission of Newbury Weekly News)

Trustees and representatives of various organisations and companies were introduced to her and she was shown the original charter of 1596 and Borough Ordinances of 1599. She was then entertained by pupils from Speenhamland Primary School performing a Tudor dance, accompanied by musicians from Park House School. Following this she walked in the Market Place. Later, the Queen visited Clere School at Burghclere and the Newbury Mencap Centre in Enborne Road.

Newbury in Wartime

At the beginning of the century, the Boer War was still being fought. A small contingent of twenty volunteers from the Newbury area were in South Africa as part of the Berkshire Yeomanry. When they returned on 10th June 1901, under their commander Colonel Ricardo, of Donnington, the townspeople turned out to cheer them back home. Members of Newbury Volunteer Fire Brigade pulled Col Ricardo's carriage from the railway station to the Market Place (whilst the other men followed in horse-drawn vehicles) where the Mayor formally welcomed them all. A triumphal arch had been erected across the road leading to Donnington.

The 1914-18 war saw many Newbury men killed; there are 330 names (including one woman) on the memorial outside St Nicolas' church. During the war the library's reading room was much used as newspapers were the only source of information and people anxiously scanned the casualty lists. Many civilians, including women, were employed in war work. It was women who made large brass shell cases at Plenty's diesel engine works. Others were employed at a temporary hospital in Oxford Street and local people also packed ammunition at Newbury Racecourse. At times mounted troops were also based there and postcards depict their encampments in the centre of the course. The racecourse was also used for a prisoner of war camp and tank repair park. The tanks used to be driven up to Greenham Common for testing.

When the Second World War was declared on 3rd September 1939, parts of the racecourse were immediately requisitioned and a RASC main supply depot set up. However, racing was able to continue until 1941 as the racecourse itself was not affected. In 1942 the USA joined the war and the rest of the racecourse was taken over. The course itself was protected with thick coconut matting and loads of soil and ash, on top of which thirty-five miles of railway track were laid to form a marshalling yard for the American Army. Petrol was stored there for the landings in North Africa. Later, all manner of equipment including Bailey bridges were kept there in readiness for the D-Day landing and invasion of Europe. Part of the course was again used as a prisoner of war camp and some wall paintings by an Austrian, Karl Schulz, still survive. These were rediscovered in 1990, the artist was also traced in Vienna and brought to Newbury to see them again.

There were changes, too, in the manufacturing businesses in the area. It is believed that Plenty's made submarine engines and that Newbury Diesel Company continued to make ship's engines. As already mentioned, Elliott's of Newbury switched from furniture making to providing parts for aircraft. Firstly these were of wood, which they were used to working, but

Newbury Racecourse in camp, 1915.

later they acquired new skills to work with aluminium alloy. They were obviously successful as the company was used in several official films showing how the aircraft sections were made. It was also visited by the Minister of Supply, Stafford Cripps. A new factory was built at Shaw for Supermarine Vickers, where fuselages for Spitfire fighters were made. The building still exists and is the headquarters for Quantel. The government had a policy of dividing up aircraft manufacture into fairly small units, so that production could continue even if some were bombed. Many small engineering firms and even motor garages were used to make small parts. Opperman Gears' move to Newbury at the beginning of the war was to remove them from the prime target of London.

Other civilians and materials also came to Newbury which was seen as a relatively safe place. Staff from the Shell offices and from the Great Western Railway were amongst them. The Lord Mayor of London's ceremonial coach was kept in the malthouse of the former Newbury Brewery in Northbrook Street and early printed books from the St Bride's Printing Library were stored in the basement of Newbury Library. Helen Purvis (the Librarian) recalled that a member of staff had packed a note with the books saying that they wished they were coming too! Many

Former POW Karl Schulz revisits Newbury in 1990 to see again the murals he painted in 1944 at The Stable Cottages, Newbury Racecourse. (Reproduced by kind permission of Newbury Weekly News)

strangers did arrive in the town, refugees from the Continent and children and adults from target areas such as Kent and Southampton as well as London. The Godolphin and Latymer school moved here from Hammersmith and shared the Girl's High School: one school used it in the mornings, the other in the afternoons. A few wealthy people spent much of the war at the Chequers Hotel. Military units too moved in, not only to the large private houses such as Shaw, Benham and Donnington Castle House, but also to places such as the Technical Institute. Official child evacuees were allocated to families in Newbury and the surrounding villages. Volunteers set up a British Restaurant and the Baptist Church Hall was used as a synagogue for the Jewish people who had come to the town. Later, a social club for the American forces was set up in the Wesleyan Hall and adjoining Day Schools.

At the beginning of the war the military were aware that Newbury

Bridge, on the main route from the Midlands to the south coast ports, was a key point. If it was destroyed then strategic delays would ensue. Therefore an emergency bridge was erected at the southern end of Parkway, using large girders delivered for the Maidenhead by-pass, which had then been cancelled at the outbreak of the war. In relatively recent years this has mistakenly been called the American Bridge. This seems to owe its origin to the US military authorities rubber-stamping the plans of the bridge much later in the war, presumably indicating that they had examined them and knew the bridge's limitations. In 2001 that bridge has finally gone and its replacement was opened on 20th July. Whilst bridging the Kennet was important, using the river and canal as a defence in case of invasion was also vital. This waterway, with the Thames, formed a moat across southern England. Concrete 'pillbox' gun emplacements were rapidly erected along the whole length of this 'moat', with especially strong defences at most bridging points. Many of these still survive. In the town itself many concrete blocks were prepared – some cylindrical, others 'dragon's teeth' or cubes. These were to be used to block roads or open areas against invading vehicles. In addition there were semi-fixed defences on the main roads into the town from the south.

The population had to endure shortages; rationing of food and fuel; the blackout; long working hours; and then additional duties such as fire watching, Home Guard or other Civil Defence operations. They were required to carry gas-masks at all times; they also had air-raid shelters to build or use (public ones remain in Station Road and north of the kiosk in Victoria Park, but windows have been put in so that they are suitable for present use) and window glass to cross-tape in case it was broken. And, not least, was the dread of hearing bad news about those in the armed forces. As with the rest of the country, people put up with the hardship and inconvenience and there was a very real feeling of community. When there was the opportunity, people played hard and enjoyed themselves. There were entertainments at the Corn Exchange, perhaps most notably when Major Glenn Miller and his swing orchestra performed there in 1944 and which was relayed outside to the crowds in the Market Place. Sadly, this was one of the last concerts he gave before his plane was lost when crossing the English Channel.

Air-raid sirens sounded on 244 occasions during the war and there was some bombing in and around Newbury, but this was not very serious, until a fateful day in February 1943. Late in the afternoon of Wednesday, the 10th, a single Dornier 217E bomber approached from the south-west and broke out of the cloud over Wash Water. It opened fire with its machine guns as it flew over Monks Lane and Newtown Road and dropped five 250kg bombs. These hit St John's church, St Bartholomew's Almshouses (Fair Close is now on their site), the Senior Council Schools, a railway signal box and one bomb which did not explode ended in the yard of the Falkland Arms. Bryan Philpott, an experienced military

February 1943. A view looking south at the damage caused by the German air attack. One bomb seriously damaged the Newbury Senior Council School seen on the other side of the railway embankment. Another clipped the edge of the signal box before exploding in the bank from where the photograph was subsequently taken. The signalman was unhurt but lucky as the spoon in the mug of tea he was drinking at the time was bent double by a brick splinter. (H.H. Dennis)

historian, believed it most likely that the plane had planned to hit Plenty's factory, as this was during a period of strategic bombing. The church, almshouses and school were destroyed and fifteen people were killed, nine in the almshouses, a corporation carpenter, a cleaner and three children in the school. The headmaster, his wife and an education secretary were badly injured, but several other people had miraculous escapes. It was fortunate that all but a few pupils had already left the school for the day. The town had suffered from an earlier disaster when one of Newbury's fire engines was sent to help with the blitz on Portsmouth in 1941. As it was entering the naval dockyard a bomb exploded and three Newbury men were killed. Crowds lined Northbrook Street to pay their respects when the coffins were carried on fire engines in a joint funeral procession.

Greenham Common

Possibly the longest lasting effect of the war on Newbury was the creation of an airfield on Greenham Common. The common had been a favourite place for Newbury people to visit, picnic and play and is remembered as a beautiful area. However, parts had been used for military purposes in past centuries. There had been exercises and manoeuvres there from at least the mid-18th century, a rifle range had been created during the 19th century and practice trenches had been dug in the first war. Even the inn on the common was called The Volunteer. Early in the war the airfield was built as a training base for RAF pilots, but later it became a base for the US 101st Airborne Division, the 'Screaming Eagles'. As D-Day approached the base became more and more crowded with aircraft and large troop-carrying gliders. On the eve of D-Day General Eisenhower, Supreme Commander and later to be President of the USA, visited the base with Winston Churchill and made the famous speech when he sent the airborne troops on their way to Victory. Newbury people had grown accustomed to the constant practice flights of the planes and the gliders they towed, but on 6th June 1944, they were nowhere to be seen and people guessed that the invasion had begun.

After the war the airfield was vacated and the people of Newbury began to hope that they would soon have their common returned to them.

Then it was announced that the airfield was to be enlarged and in 1950 the road across the common was closed and a new route to Kingsclere built from the Swan Inn, Newtown along the southern fringe of the common, to pick up the old route near Knights Bridge.

In 1951 the USAF were back, this time with B47 jet bombers, widely believed to be armed with atomic bombs. This story gained credence through the strengthening of the defences around the armament compound in Drayton's Gully. In the late 1970s the Ministry of Defence said that giant jet-powered tanker aircraft were to be based at Greenham. This caused a huge protest in the area, particularly as the flight path crossed the now densely populated southern part of Newbury, including several schools. There was great fear of the devastation which would be caused if one of these loaded tankers crashed. After all there had been a number of accidents involving aircraft from the base. There was a change of mind and the tankers were moved to Fairford, Gloucestershire instead.

For a time, use of the base was at a low intensity, then in 1981 it was announced that Greenham was to have Tomahawk Cruise Missiles with

Greenham Common. Demonstrators against the Cruise Missiles link hands in an attempt to encircle the airfield, April 1983. (Reproduced by kind permission of Newbury Weekly News)

nuclear warheads based there. This provoked horror, not only locally, but nationwide and subsequently worldwide, as the Women's Peace Protest movement caught international attention.

There were many who thought that a strong defence against the perceived threat from the Communist bloc was required and that the women were a threat to our national defence. Whatever one's belief, Newbury and Greenham Common gained worldwide notoriety and the women received financial and moral support from all corners of the globe. They received less support from the local community and from some quarters there was strong opposition. Many who lived around the base thought that the value of their property would be reduced through the squalid condition of the camps and activities of the women and their repeated damage to the strong perimeter fence being erected.

To be fair to the protesters, most held a very strong belief in their reasons for opposing deployment of the missiles and lived very uncomfortable lives. The Ministry of Defence and Newbury District Council were of the opinion that the protesters had no right to be there and constantly evicted them from land, destroyed their shelters and confiscated their possessions. Many women were taken to court repeatedly and fined or sent to prison. Despite this a core of women stayed year after year, with others joining them for days or months.

Whilst the protest went on, the work to create the silos for the missile convoys and the control buildings was completed. The missiles and their transport and control vehicles were delivered by giant aircraft, whose distinctive whine became a familiar sound. The first missiles, of an eventual 106, arrived in November 1983. As the conveys were sent out on exercise the women and their supporters attacked them and followed them to ensure their movements could not be secret. Then, quite suddenly, it seemed, there was agreement between the USSR and the West that the number of strategic weapons and nuclear devices should be reduced. As part of the agreement (Intermediate Nuclear Forces Treaty) the missiles were returned to the USA to be destroyed, the final ones going in March 1991. The last of the US forces left the base in September 1992 and the following year the Ministry of Defence announced its sale. After complexities concerned with the rights of Commoners were tested in the courts, the Ministry agreed to sell the land at a price less than they had originally hoped for. As referred to earlier, Greenham Common Trust purchased it for seven million pounds and it is being restored to natural heathland. After military fixtures such as fuel tanks had been removed or made safe, the fence was removed and the public given access to all of the common (except the silos) on 8th April 2000. The last of the Greenham Women protesters left on 7th September 2000, the nineteenth anniversary of their arrival.

So ends the story of Newbury – so far. At the beginning of the new millennium the town is prosperous, though its development has brought new pressures to be resolved. But Newbury has completed its successful transition from local market town to a modern business and distribution centre, it remains within a setting of beautiful countryside and is a pleasant place to live. No one knows what the future may bring, but surely the mix of skilled managers, entrepreneurs, scientific, technical and artistic people who live here will ensure its continuing success.

---------------CHAPTER EIGHT---------------

The Architectural Heritage

A short description of the more interesting buildings of Newbury and six architecturally significant ones in its immediate neighbourhood, are given in the following pages. Attention is concentrated on buildings erected before the late 19th century and confined to those in the central area of the town. After the introduction, streets are followed generally from north to south. Those who wish to use the descriptions as a basis for a tour of the town may find the map on pages 74 and 75 useful.

The map is based on a copy by Brian Coghlan of an 18th century map of Newbury, and is in the collections of West Berkshire Museum. In redrawing the map for this book Max Breach has superimposed modern roads. However, it should be noted that the main roads out of the town have not been severely re-aligned as indicated, but that their angle was inaccurately shown in 1768. This applies similarly to the present Bear Lane (south of Market Place), Northcroft Lane, Newtown Road and Derby Road (off Argyle Road). In 1768, Wash Lane crossed what is now the City Recreation Ground and led to Andover, although a new road had by then been built on the line of the present road from St John's roundabout to Chandos Road.

Introduction

Buildings can have a long life and whilst when erecting a modern building the site is totally cleared before work starts, in the past any useable parts of an existing building would be incorporated into the new one. Sometimes, only the facade of a building would be changed, to bring

Northbrook Street from the bridge, 1851. (West Berkshire Museum)

Northbrook Street from the bridge, 2001.

it up to date. For example, the Northbrook Street frontage of Jack of Newbury's house once had a jettied first floor and gable. When the building next to White Hart House was being demolished so that the Royal Bank of Scotland could be extended, elaborately moulded timbers from a 15th century house were found to be embedded in the 18th century brick front-age. Likewise, several buildings in the town centre may be found to conceal older structures behind 18th or 19th century frontages. The descriptions which follow will concentrate on the external appearance of buildings.

Before the street by street listing, a summary of the most important or typical buildings of each period will be given. From this it will be seen that Newbury is particularly rich in good 18th century houses and also has a significant group of Gothic-influenced buildings; both 18th and 19th century versions. This is headed by the outstanding Donnington Grove. Sandleford Priory is also by one of the leading architects using this style. From an earlier period, Shaw House is a fine Elizabethan manor house and probably the most important secular building in the area. Its design then inspired the design of Greenham Lodge, the closest to Newbury of several buildings by leading 19th century architects. An indication of the influences on the architectural style of the 18th century and later buildings is given in brackets after their names.

Medieval Buildings (All buildings visibly of this period are listed)
Donnington Castle was built around 1330/40 as a fortified house, rather
 than a strong defensive work. Surviving gateway 1386. See also page 27.
House of c1500, rear of 50, Northbrook Street.
Jack of Newbury's House, Northbrook Street. See page 34.
Litten Chapel, Newtown Road – junction with Pound Street. See page 25.

Tudor and Elizabethan Buildings
St Nicolas' church, c1530. See page 36.
Shaw House, Church Lane, Shaw, c1581. See page 39.
Old Eight Bells, Bartholomew Street, 16th century.

Jacobean and Other 17th Century Buildings
Cloth Hall (Museum), Wharf Street, 1626/7.
Camp Hopson, Northbrook Street, 1663 building.
St Bartholomew's Almshouses, Argyle Road, 1618, clocktower 1698.
Coxedd's Almshouses, West Mills, late 17th (possibly early 18th)
 century.

18th Century

Donnington Grove, John Chute c1760 ('Strawberry Hill' Gothic).

Benham Park 1772/5, Lancelot 'Capability' Brown & Henry Holland (Classical).

Sandleford House, James Wyatt 1780/1 (Gothic) (Oval room with lobbies, Classical).

Thames Court, Broadway, c1700 (Classical).

5, Wharf Street, early 18th century (Classical).

Chestnuts, Old Bath Road, possibly 1720 (Classical).

42, Northbrook Street, 1724 (possibly Spanish Netherlands).

91/92, Northbrook Street, early-mid 18th century (Classical).

St Nicolas' House, West Mills, mid 18th century (Classical).

Phoenix House, Bartholomew Street, early-mid 18th century (Classical).

Goldwell House, Old Bath Road, possibly 1740 (Classical) (additional floor later).

Albion House, 27, Oxford Street, mid-18th century (Classical).

Churchyard Gates, Bartholomew Street, c1770 (Gothic).

St Mary's House, London Road, late 18th century (Gothic).

63, Cheap Street, 1796 (bow windows early 19th century).

Industrial: Granary, The Wharf

                Maltings, Inch's Yard.

19th Century

Cottages, Shaw Road, 1818 & Smith's Terrace, 1823 (Vernacular/ Classical).

The Shrubbery, 22, Oxford Road, early 19th century (Classical).

St Mary's Place, early 19th century (Gothic).

Upper Raymonds', see Derby Road, 1826 (Gothic).

St Nicolas School, Enborne Road, William Butterfield, 1859 (Gothic).

Town Hall, Market Place, 1878 (Gothic).

Corn Exchange, Market Place, J.S. Dodd, 1861/2 (Italianate).

National Westminster Bank, Market Place, 1864 (Italian-Gothic).

Greenham Lodge, Norman Shaw, 1875 (Elizabethan).

Grammar School, Enborne Road, Power & Hughes, 1885 (Tudor).

Post Office, Cheap Street, 1896 (Tudor).

Industrial: Phoenix Brewery, Bartholomew Street

                7, Cheap Street (seed warehouse).

20th Century Churches

St George's, Wash Common, F.C. Eden, 1933 & John Griffin, 1965
  (Italianate).

St John's, Newtown Road, S.E. Dykes-Bower, 1956 (Roman influenced).

Buildings Outside Newbury

Donnington Castle, Donnington was built around 1330/40 as a fortified house, rather than a strong defensive work; the surviving gateway is from 1386. During the Civil War it was the earthwork defences and gun emplacements which provided its strength. Parts of these can still be seen. The castle is in the care of English Heritage and the exterior can always be seen.

Shaw House, Church Lane, Shaw. The largest Elizabethan mansion in Berkshire, built of brick with a stone porch and dressings, completed c1581. Not open for visitors as currently awaiting restoration and within the campus of Trinity School, but its south front can be seen from Church Lane.

Donnington Grove, Grove Road, Donnington. The house was designed by John Chute who was a friend of Horace Walpole and had helped with the design of his house, Strawberry Hill, Twickenham a few years earlier. That house had led the revival of interest in Gothic design and gave its name to a particular Gothic style, which Donnington Grove follows. Motifs of clustered slender columns and shallow pointed arches are repeated throughout the house. The house is a private country club with restaurant and golf course, which presents opportunities for seeing the house. From time to time there are also public events in the grounds or house.

Sandleford Priory, off the A339, south of Newbury. Originally the house was a small medieval priory which became a private house. It was remodelled for Mrs Elizabeth Montagu, the noted blue-stocking, by James Wyatt in 1780–81. He, too, followed a Gothic style, though blending it with classical influences so far as the exterior was concerned. He used round and square headed windows, castellated the parapets and added crocketts and pinnacles. The interior varies, the hall is frankly Gothic, but the oval drawing room at the rear, which is separated from other parts by small, rectangular, pillared lobbies, has a domed ceiling and is decorated in a

Donnington Grove. (Author)

Benham House. (Author)

classical Adam style. The Priory is now a private girl's school, St Gabriel's, and there is no public admittance, except for occasional events held in the grounds.

Benham House (also known as Benham Valence) was built for the sixth Earl of Craven in 1772/5 by Lancelot 'Capability' Brown and his son-in-law, Henry Holland. The house is a large stone-built Classical building of three storeys with a portico of four unfluted Ionic columns and no pediment. The top of the portico and roof of the house have balustraded parapets. Following military use during the 1939-45 war, the house was neglected and in a dilapidated state. The house was restored by Norsk Data in 1983-5 (which also involved demolishing a later extension). Norsk Data (now part of Nextra) now occupy modern offices in the grounds and the mansion belongs to Prudential and is let to Prime Business Solutions. There is access to the grounds only to people who have business with tenants. The gatepiers and lodges at the north-east entrance from the A4 are also of excellent design.

Greenham Lodge (Mary Hare Primary School), Pigeons Farm Road, Greenham was built in 1875 for Lloyd H. Baxendale, by R. Norman Shaw, a leading 19th century architect. The external design is influenced by Shaw House, but the architect has made it his own with features such as the enormous windows to the short wings either side of the entrance. The interior too is original with a high hall, overlooked by a gallery with oriel windows. There are immense chimney pieces in several rooms, originally decorated with William de Morgan and other decorative tiles, some of which remain. Again there is no public access, but the facade can easily be seen from the road.

Although it may not be possible to see these notable local buildings, in the past they are likely to have influenced builders and architects in the area and thus to have affected the designs of local buildings. Books giving accounts of 'Grand Tours' to Italy and Greece, published drawings etc and publication of ideas about architecture also had a great influence on building design from the 17th century onwards.

Buildings in the Town:
A Street by Street Guide

OLD BATH ROAD

Castle Houses, opposite the beginning of Speen Lane, was formerly the famous Castle Inn. It is a large building of three storeys, the west part is early 18th century, the eastern a little later, the whole front is stuccoed. The building underwent considerable alteration in the 19th century, when it was converted into three houses. Part was later turned into flats.

The Lawn (Merant) has a good early 18th century front, this is the right hand section of the building which is five windows wide. The left hand section is the first extension built for Kleinworth Benson; the later, much larger one, is to the rear.

'Goldwell' (Graphico) is some way further along and on the opposite side of the road. It is said to have been built about 1740, but the fine staircase appears to be of the late 17th century. There is a projecting section with a pediment to the west elevation, but the top floor seems to be a later addition to the building. Although the house appears cramped in its site one has to remember that originally it sat in spacious gardens now partly occupied by a housing estate and recreation land linking to Northcroft. The house is now used as offices but at one time was the home of the Page family. Francis Page was a successful trader and in 1768 purchased all the shares of the Kennet Navigation. (See page 69).

Speen Court (Vodafone). This building was originally a lovely mid to late 18th century house of variegated brick, ornamented with brick pilasters and a moulded cornice. It appears that it was built with two storeys and that a third has been added above the cornice; the large bow window to the west elevation is an addition of the Regency period. If the doorway facing the road was the main entrance, then it would have had an elaborate doorcase in scale with the house.

Further east stands The Chestnuts, 2, Old Bath Road (Future Link) a very fine early Georgian house. The date 1720 appears on the roof, but the building is more in the earlier Queen Anne style. It is built of variegated brick and is of two storeys, with attic rooms and cellars. The south front has a pediment and there are decorative details in the brickwork, whilst the window heads are of rubbed brick with very narrow mortar joints. A large old chestnut tree was felled in 1928, but in recent years a horse chestnut has been planted to perpetuate the name.

Opposite The Chestnuts are two interesting buildings. The High House, as its name implies, is a tall building of three floors and a basement. Built mid to late 18th century of red brick, there are round-headed recesses to the first floor into which the windows are set. There is a small cornice to the parapet which hides the roof and a Tuscan porch with columns at the top of a short flight of steps.

Queen Anne House, number 35. This building looks as if it dates from the 17th century (ie earlier than Queen Anne) and seems to have had an extra floor added above the original moulded brick eaves cornice. For some years up to the 1980s the building was divided into two houses, but the right hand front door has been successfully restored to a window. The entrance is unusually high above the pavement, which one can only assume was to give the basement more height.

OXFORD ROAD

Wessex House, number 22 (formerly named The Shrubbery) is a neat early 19th century Regency house, now offices. It is of two storeys, stuccoed to give a plain finish but with Ionic pilasters and a moulded cornice; a small parapet modifies the roof line. Across the front is an iron trellis veranda with a concave roof, shading the French windows of the ground floor.

OXFORD STREET

The north side of this street, stretching to where Wheelers garage now stands in London Road, was where the coaching inns were concentrated and almost mid-way between London and Bath. Until the building of the railways it was a busy, bustling area.

Firstly, on the south side of the road, number 27, Albion House is another fine mid-18th century building of variegated brick. The expanse of the wide front is relieved by the side bays being slightly recessed. The shape of the rubbed brick window heads differs on each floor, with a feature being made of the tall central window of the first floor which has a semi circular head whilst the others are segmental. Those of the ground floor have large keystones linking the horizontal string course. The slate roof with its deep eaves is an early 19th century replacement.

The Bacon Arms appears as a late 18th century building from its exterior, but remains of timber framing inside indicates its earlier origin. The arched entrance for coaches to reach the inn yard has been brought into the hotel to form its entrance lobby.

The Chequers, another former coaching inn, has been extensively altered, incorporating a house between it and the Bacon Arms as well as modern buildings to the rear. An entrance to the coach yard – now car park – exists through the eastern wing of the hotel. It is unclear whether this originally formed part of the Chequers or if it was a separate building.

Number 4 (Best of Bikes) is a three storey 18th century red brick house with a dentilled brick cornice below the roof. The ground floor was faced with rusticated stucco, imitating a stone building, in the 19th century. A carriage way gives access to the yard and although strictly there is no right of way, one can obtain an impression here of the appearance of the old coach yards. The buildings to the east side of the yard are the remains of Adnams Brewery, established in 1802, though it had been a brewery before that date. The rear building is timber framed and likely to date from the early 18th century at least. One of the buildings on the west side is said to be part of a 17th century malthouse. Some of its timbers can be seen from the Chequers yard entrance.

BROADWAY

Forming a roundabout in the centre is the Clock House or Clock Tower, built in 1929 and looking like a market cross. On its triangular turret, above the clock faces, are depictions of previous structures on this spot. The earliest is the gas lamp on a stone column base, erected by public subscription in 1828 (now moved to Old Bath Road/Speen Lane junction). Then in 1889 an elaborate iron lamp post and clock to mark Queen Victoria's Jubilee in 1887. The lamps were later replaced with free-standing lamps, as illustrated in the photograph on the next page.

Numbers 26 and 24 (Khan Tandoori and Threshers) were formerly The Bear Inn (did the inn once extend to include Best of Bikes, or was its

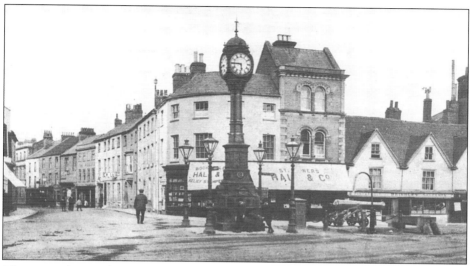

The Broadway, facing London Road, c1905.

entrance through number 26 which is an extension to 24?). The building has a mid to late 18th century brick front with a moulded and dentilled brick cornice below the parapet. Above the first floor windows is a continuous moulded string course.

Thames Court (formerly York House) and the three buildings to the east (Vodafone) mark the famous George and Pelican Inn. Because of later alterations it is not clear how much of the three eastern buildings remain from their days as an inn, except that where they turn at right angles to London Road is the entrance to the Pelican's stables. Thames Court is one of the town's most notable buildings, dating from at least the very early 18th century. At first floor level the windows have triangular and segmental pediments in pairs, between the second floor windows are dwarf pilasters on enriched corbels and above these a modillioned (small brackets) eaves cornice at roof level. The ground floor had been converted to a bank and a shop, but the building was restored in about 1980, when the two doorways were installed – but one is false.

Number 19 – west side of Broadway – (Dovetail Employment Agency) is an 18th century house with original Georgian shop front. There has been some restoration of the bowed shop windows and most of the glass is modern, but it is a delightful survival. Adjoining the shop is a passageway, Saddlers Court, named after the business carried out at the premises for many years. This leads to several much-restored old cottages and outbuildings, but there are interesting details of tile-hanging etc.

Further down towards Northbrook Street the Broadway narrows. This marks the old boundary between the parishes of Newbury and Speen and therefore of the area of the latter known as Speenhamland. The infamous 'Speenhamland Act' derived its name from the meeting of the Berkshire magistrates held at the George and Pelican Inn in May 1795 (see page 76). The boundary was formed by the Northbrook, which was a branch of the River Kennet that flowed across Northcroft and then through Victoria Park before rejoining the main channel.

On the east side of the road is The King's Coffee House (Waud), which probably dates from the 17th century but its exterior has been much altered, particularly the ground floor.

LONDON ROAD

The buildings of the western section of the road have been much altered (but see above for the George and Pelican Inn) though no doubt several have ancient cores and there are Georgian fronts to some of those on the south side. The Cross Keys is a 19th century building which replaced the well-known coaching inn of that name.

The first buildings of note are almost opposite Park Way.

Number 34, Manor House is of two storeys with three attic dormer windows. It has an early 18th century stuccoed front with a moulded eaves cornice, though the core is 17th century or earlier. The five first floor windows have 18th or early 19th century sashes, but the porch is a modern replacement.

Number 40, St Mary's House (Antony Gorley & Co/Newbury Business Centre) is one of Newbury's late 18th century Gothic buildings, the frontage of grey brick, the rest red brick (the rear wall is 19th century). It is the form of the stone-framed windows and doorway, together with the cornice and battlements to the parapet, which give the building its Gothic appearance. Note the ogee arch and slender tripartite shafts of the doorway, typical Gothic features; the original small pinnacles above the shafts eroded and those present are replacements. Pineapples are certainly an 18th century design motif, but the carving of the finial at the top of the doorway looks too crisp to be original.

Clarendon House (Swinton Insurance) is a good 18th century building – the date 1750 or '59 is on a brick. It was built as an extension to the famous King's Arms Inn (later the Dower House) demolished in 1956. It has been suggested that it was built by James Clarke who built Newbury Bridge and the Mansion House. The shop windows are a modern alteration. The c1990 building (Dower House – Vodafone) on the site of the King's Arms was designed to echo the form of the old inn.

Beyond the Robin Hood roundabout is the inn which gave it its name. Originally a private house, The Myrtles, it was purchased as a replacement for the beerhouse next door, when that was demolished in the 1970s so that the roundabout could be built. The Robin Hood (Harvester) is a large early 19th century house of grey and variegated brick with rubbed and

St Mary's House, 40, London Road.

gauged brick window heads under a hipped slate roof with deep eaves. Across the front is an iron framed veranda with a concave leaded roof.

The description of buildings in London Road is continued after Shaw Road.

SHAW ROAD

It is possible to use the underpass adjacent to number 107 London Road to reach Shaw Road. Most of the attractive terraced houses here are of early 19th century date; whilst at first glance they appear identical, there is variation. Some are one room wide whilst others are double-fronted; several have cellars. They were built at different times, the group with the archway (Smith's Crescent) is dated 1823 and 75-79 are dated 1818.

To the north of all of these and next to the River Lambourn, is number 107. This is a substantial 18th century house, but based on an earlier core, perhaps 16th century; the tile-hung gable looks 17th century. (Cottages converted from the buildings of Shaw Mill are almost opposite, but are not included here as they are in Shaw cum Donnington parish.)

LONDON ROAD – SOUTH SIDE

At the south-west corner of the roundabout is –
107 London Road, an early 19th century house of red and blue brick, beneath a hipped slate roof with overhanging eaves. The ground floor door and windows are set in shallow round-arched recesses, a feature that first appears in 18th century buildings, spreading to smaller houses in the early 19th century.

Next door is St Joseph's Presbytery of similar date, less decorative but still handsome, followed by the first Catholic church here, of 1864.

The Roman Catholic church of St Joseph was completed in 1928. It is built in the Italian basilican style and has a detached campanile. The building was designed by W.C. Mangan and was built by local firm Hoskins and Pond.

Between the church and St Mary's Road is a pair of semi-detached tall and large mid-late Victorian houses.

Just beyond the modern buildings (on the site of the church) at the corner of St Mary's Road are 77 and 75 London Road, a pair of three storey stucco villas of about 1830/40; note the false windows in the centre, added to aid the building's symmetry. The recessed side bays of two storeys appear to be original features, as does the projecting porch of number 75, but the bay window is a later addition. The shallow-pitched roof is of slate and has deep eaves.

ST MARY'S PLACE/VICTORIA PARK

Return towards the roundabout and turn right into St Mary's Road, enter Victoria Park and follow the footpath to the right. From this one can see the end of a terrace of white painted, early 19th century Gothic houses in St Mary's Place. Access to these is via a private footpath. From the park can be seen the end house, set at right angles to the others; it has three windows of paired Gothic sashes under flat window heads with dripmoulds; buttresses rise above the parapet. The entrance to each house is by a recessed porch with Gothic ogee dripmould. The three houses furthest from the park have three storeys, the others two storeys, two with attics.

There are other cottages facing the park, early 19th century near the end of St Mary's Road and late 19th century approaching Park Way. All are attractive.

NORTHBROOK STREET

Continue along the footpath to Park Way; opposite and slightly to the right is Park Street. Walk down here and on the right immediately before Northbrook Street is a small courtyard (Northbrook Court).

A house of c1500 can be seen at the far side. This structure was destined for demolition in 1988 when 50 Northbrook Street was to be refurbished. Fortunately Berkshire County Council's conservation specialist recognised what it was and it, too, was restored. It is a rare survival in this area of a timber-framed medieval town dwelling. Although it is relatively plain and much smaller than Jack of Newbury's House (see below) it would have been the home of a prosperous man.

Turn right into Northbrook Street to the front of –

50 Northbrook Street (Potamus, Bradley & Willows, Software Exchange). For many years this was the premises of one of Newbury's leading provision merchants, J. Webb & Sons. In the late 1980s, when the building

Conservation in practice. The redevelopment of Nos 49/50 Northbrook Street in 1988 revealed a beautiful example of a half timbered dwelling dating back to around 1500. Demolition of what was described in the Planning Application as an 'old barn' was refused and the building was subsequently blended successfully into the new development (see picture opposite). The picture above shows the house as it appeared in July 1988 (Newbury Weekly News/Peter Bloodworth)

was stripped down to its frame and restored, it was seen that at an earlier time it had been two or more buildings, which had been unified by the decorative tile-hung front. Tile-hanging was once a widespread feature of local properties, usually to improve the weather proofing of buildings where the bricks or wattle and daub were porous, or to cover such unfashionable materials. It was often used for gables or dormers which were more exposed. Of course, its decorative potential was also appreciated as in this building. It seems most often to have been used in the 17th and 18th centuries.

The Monument Inn is opposite; although it appears to be built of brick there is much evidence of timber framing inside, along with the form of the roof this points to it being built in the 17th century, at least. The window frames, bargeboards and tile-hanging of the dormers have all been changed in the past century. However, it remains one of Newbury's more complete old buildings.

The Methodist church stands back from the street and is an interesting building of 1837/8, with lancet windows being a particular feature of the design.

To the south of the church the building now occupied by Hampton's International and Infinity was Newbury's second cinema, opening in 1910, a few weeks after the first one. The oddly roofed construction at first floor level was the projection room which, because of the flammability of film, had to be separated from the auditorium.

Bakers Sound and Vision is almost opposite the church and is another of

Newbury's early 19th century buildings with windows set into an arched recess.

Number 42 (Specsavers) is a most unusual and ornate building. Its date, 1724, is clear but its influences less so – nor is the monogram (presumably of its owner) easy to unravel. It has been suggested that the architectural influence is from the Netherlands, from their period of Spanish rule, but how it came to be created here is still undiscovered. Small statues representing the four seasons formerly stood on the parapet, flanking the raised central section.

On the same side Going Places is an early 18th century building, and 33 and 34 (Sportserve and Jones & Son) is one three storey building with four venetian windows, probably late 18th century. Opposite, number 66/67 (Jessops) and 70 (Lawrence's) are probably late 17th/early 18th century, through somewhat altered.

Number 26 (Cheltenham & Gloucester) has a mid to late 18th century front of red brick. The upper sections of two Doric pilasters rise up through the

Number 42, Northbrook Street, dated 1724.

moulded brick cornice to support the raised central pediment of the parapet. The four first floor windows have moulded architraves and keystones. The building behind the frontage is earlier in date with a hipped tiled roof.

We now reach Marsh Lane, the pedestrian passageway which provides the view of the northern gable of Jack of Newbury's House (Monsoon). This elaborately decorated timber-framed building dates from the 15th century (see page 34) and once stretched over the site now occupied by Lunn Poly and Marks & Spencer – and possibly further. If you look at the edge of the wall behind the modern shop fronts, evidence that the first floor and roof were once jettied out (similarly to the northern gable) can be seen. Comparison of the scale of this house with the c1500 house seen from Park Street indicates the status and wealth of Jack.

A passageway through the building opposite Marks & Spencer is the entrance to Cromwell Place. On the right of this is a row of mid-18th century cottages with rubbed brick window heads. When there were converted to offices in 1959 some doorways were transformed into windows. On the south side the cottages are mid or late 18th century, with surrounds added to the windows when the Congregational schoolroom was built in 1856. There is an interesting detail about these. At some time the surface of the bricks must have been weathered and a thin skim of coloured cement was applied with narrow bands of false pointing – a time consuming task. Nine cottages, continuing the row, were demolished for the schoolroom to be built. At the end of Cromwell Place is the United Reformed church with the schoolroom to the left.

Further south on the same side of Northbrook Street is number 91/92 (Vision Express and, at present, Olivers Timpson). Above the shop fronts can be seen the upper floors of an 18th century house. The brickwork is of very high quality, the front being constructed from rubbed bricks, with very fine mortar joints. It is seven windows wide and three storeys high, decorated with eight tall pilasters which pass through the cornice to support the parapet. Some of the segmental arched windows retain their original glazing bars dividing the windows into twelve panes, but others have been blocked up. There are references to a rainwater head being dated 1774, but the building is forty or fifty years earlier.

Camp Hopson occupy several old buildings, but the central one is the

The central portion of the Camp Hopson range of buildings, dated 1663.

jewel. Number 8 is dated 1663. It is one of the most notable and beautiful town houses in England and also a very early example of rubbed brickwork. Each of the two storeys above the shop front has four windows and is ornamented with Doric and Ionic pilasters. There is a modillioned eaves cornice of moulded bricks, below the paired tile-hung gables. Inside there is a good staircase with its original ceiling. This is decorated with an egg and tongue cornice and a cherub medallion at its centre. The other buildings which flank this are both of late 18th century date and worthy of attention.

Number 94 (Dixons) is opposite; its front is 18th and 19th century, but the building is a 17th century house and its gables can be seen at the rear.

Just past the shop Cargo, as the ramp of the bridge begins, is an opening leading to the River Kennet (used as part of the canal) from which one can see the front of the Old Rectory (Highcross), a mid-18th century building with a good doorway. This was incorporated into Toomer's hardware shop until they moved and the premises were remodelled.

Back in Northbrook Street, on the corner of Northcroft Lane opposite is the building which was formerly the Tudor Cafe (now Hadleighs and Clark's) and probably dates from that era. Many timbers can be seen inside and indicate that it was once three or four buildings and that there were once three gables to the front. At one time the first floor spanned the entrance to Northcroft Lane.

NORTHCROFT LANE

The first section of the lane is pedestrianised. On the south side is a continuation of the buildings associated with the former Tudor Cafe, though some are now incorporated with a public house by the river. On the north side, as it begins to widen, is a former brick almshouse of 1821 (part of Bowness Sports). It was endowed by John Childs, a sail-cloth maker.

Salvation Army Hall, Temperance Hall and Childs Almshouse. (Author)

The tall building which was Newbury Arts Workshop from 1979-1999 has a frontage relating to its time as the Temperance Hall, opened 1875. But inside it is clear that the structure is much older, there is timber framing with cruck beams at first floor level. From the size of floor beams and its height it is possible that it was a warehouse. In view of its later history it is interesting that in the late 18th century it was used for theatrical performances by a company of strolling players – before the theatre was built at Speenhamland.

Next door is the Salvation Army Hall, an ornate, perhaps over-decorated Victorian building of 1892. A variety of materials are used including, flint, terracotta and moulded brick.

Then one comes to a group of cottages which date from the early 19th century. Numbers 14 and 16 are of grey brick with red brick dressings, the red ones being a very rich colour. Number 16 was The Drummers beer house and also has good detailing.

BRIDGE STREET

Newbury Bridge has been described on page 70. The four buildings incorporating the decorative shelters are Costa, Newbury Building Society, Griffins and Britannia Building Society. The first three of these buildings are mid to late 18th century, Costa had an ornate iron balcony across its front until the 20th century. On the south-east corner of the bridge Birthdays, a mid 18th century building, has a three sided bay which once came down to street level. Note the Gothic design glazing bars to the central windows.

MANSION HOUSE STREET

The buildings on the north side of Mansion House Street are all of three storeys. Number 4 (The Field) is a mid 18th century building with moulded brickwork round the windows. Number 5 (British Heart Foundation) is early 18th century. The front is of red brick with segmental window heads. The south side is occupied by the Town Hall extension of 1910.

MARKET PLACE

Numbers 34 and 32 (Ask and Cafe Uno) were united as one shop in 1827 and later became Beynons, whose sign remains at roof level. They both

Market Place, with Queen Victoria's statue, c1904.

date from the mid to late 18th century though the structure is older. The two bay windows at first floor level are replacements of the late 1980s copying the originals.

The National Westminster Bank, a handsome building, was built as a bank in 1864 to a design in 'Italian Gothic' by J. Chancellor. The parapet was originally pierced and the ground floor is obviously modern.

The Old Wagon and Horses has an early 19th century stuccoed front on an early 17th century building.

White Hart House (Gardner Leader) has an early 18th century front with slightly bowed windows but the building is of an earlier period, possibly 16th century. It was once one of Newbury's leading inns and retains an ancient sign. The entrance to the inn yard was adjacent to the Cloth Hall. To the south is the Hatchet Inn, comprising two buildings, both stucco and probably of the late 19th century but on an earlier core.

The Corn Exchange of 1861–2 (see page 123) was designed by J.S. Dodd. It has a three bay front divided by Corinthian pilasters surmounted by a full width pediment.

The Queens Hotel has a 19th century front of three storeys, though earlier work is contained within the fabric. The ground floor window is of four lights separated by slender cast iron columns with decorated caps. In the mid 1990s the former coach entrance was brought within the building and an extension erected to its rear.

Returning on the west side, numbers 21 to 25 were probably two buildings but are now one, stuccoed and early 19th century in appearance. Behind this the structure is much older, possibly 17th century. During renovation in the late 1960s a lead plaque with the date 1681 was found and mounted on the outside of the building where it can still be seen. Above and north of The Arcade are two buildings restored during the 1990s. First is a three storey house and shop of red brick with a hipped tile roof, probably 18th century. Number 29 is a three storey 19th century building of red brick, with pilasters at each side which have scrolled bases. It has large paned windows and a hipped slate roof. This appears to have been built as a shop, with accommodation for the owner, as the design of the original shop front matched the architecture of the upper floors.

The Town Hall was built in 1878, the clocktower completed by 1881. The architect was James H. Money, brother of the historian; the design is characteristic of the style of Alfred Waterhouse who had built Reading Town Hall in 1872-5 (See page 89).

Cross the top of the Market Place, into –

WHARF STREET AND THE WHARF

Numbers 1 and 3 (The Hogshead) form one building with a stuccoed front of the 19th century, but behind this the structure is earlier. The building, with large auction sale rooms to the rear, was formerly the premises of Day, Shergold and Herbert.

Number 5 is a striking early 18th century building. There is a projecting string course at each floor level and an eaves cornice and pilastered parapet. The windows have segmental brick heads and stone cills. Internally there are good quality contemporary fittings, but the external doorcase is later.

On the south side is The Old Cloth Hall (West Berkshire Museum), in fact more of a cloth factory as it was built from the bequest of John Kendrick in

The Granary, The Wharf, now a part of the museum.

1626-7 (see page 41). It is only one wing of the original and it is believed that the street represents the courtyard of the building. Note the ornate brackets which support the first floor overhang. To the east is a flat roofed and gabled extension of 1934.

On the left as The Wharf is entered is Wharf House (HyPerformix), a mid-18th century two storey stuccoed house. This was once the home of the proprietor of the Wharf (see Goldwell House, Old Bath Road).

The Granary occupies the southern side. It is a long and picturesque galleried building of two storeys, most of it used by the museum. The ground floor is sheltered by the overhanging gallery which is approached by a double central staircase. This originally gave access to the individual storerooms of the first floor. The gallery is protected by an extension of the tiled roof. The ground floor was originally windowless and the building provided storerooms for traders using Newbury Wharf. In its present form the building dates from the early 18th century, which ties in with the opening of Newbury Wharf and the River Kennet Navigation in 1723.

However, some people consider it to have been modified from an earlier building. The bay windows of the ground floor were added in the 1930s.

On the far side of the Wharf is Newbury Library designed by Sutton, Griffin & Morgan and opened in 2000.

Walk back to the Market Place, turn left and continue into –

CHEAP STREET

On the east side is the Post Office built in 1896 – a Victorian Tudor building. Opposite is number 33 (Greenwoods) which is basically a remodelled 17th century building. Originally it would have been single storey with attics. The bargeboards and pendants are probably faithful copies of the original and have the initials SAM and date 1679. Number 44 (Downer & Co) is an exuberant late Victorian building probably 1870-80. It is built of grey brick with terracotta shafts dividing their first floor windows which have terracotta keystones.

Numbers 49 and 50 (Casino Slots and Harris Hair) share a striking stucco front with a very deep coved cornice. At one time the date 1637 was on this building which is realistic for its construction. A little further down on the opposite side is number 16 (The Plaice Takeaway) which has a tile-hung front and is likely to be early 18th century. The former Newbury Library was built in 1905-6 with a grant from the Carnegie Trust. It became redundant when the new library was built in 2000.

On the west side of the road number 8 (Mills & Bann) has a late 18th century variegated brick frontage, though this was painted over some years ago. On the east side number 63 (Marconi) is a most attractive building of 1796 with full height bay windows added a little after this date. The Doric doorway has a semi-circular fanlight.

Almost opposite, the Conservative Association office is an early 19th century house of red brick with yellow brick dressings and window heads. On the north side of this is the former shop and warehouse of Midwinters, seed merchant. This is an interesting late Victorian industrial building with cast iron framed windows to the side elevation.

Return to St Nicolas' church and follow the road or the footpath either side of the church into –

WEST MILLS

On the left hand side is St Nicolas' House (Youth Department of St Nicolas' church) an important mid-18th century building of two storeys, built of grey brick with red brick dressings and pilasters at the corners. The windows have semi-elliptical heads of rubbed brick and the cornice is of moulded brick with dentils. The doorway has a semi-circular fanlight and a fine pedimented hood supported by brackets with cherubs' heads. Inside there is a very good contemporary staircase with three designs of baluster to each step. Attached to this building is The Chantry, an 18th century house with later stuccoed finish. It has a very fine 18th century Doric columned porch, reputed to have originally belonged to The White Hart, Market Place.

Many of the buildings in West Mills have interest and attention will be drawn only to a few. The former Hunt Almshouses are set end-on to the road. They were built in 1817 and have Gothic detailing to the windows. Numbers 15/16 (part of Tandata Systems Ltd) are the former Coxedd's Almshouses of 17th or 18th century date, two single storey cottages with attics and a shared entrance. Next but one is the former Pearce's

Weavers' Cottages, West Mills, c1904.

Almshouses, founded in 1672, but the timbered building must be older, the sash windows with dripmoulds above are 18th century. Number 22, named The Club House, is on the corner of Kennet Road. It is a fine building of the early 18th century. Built of red brick it has a moulded string course at first floor level and a moulded eaves cornice. The entrance is a modern replacement, but an indication of the scale of the original doorcase is given by the shaping of the string course. Across the road, the end of Weavers' Cottages can be seen, tile-hung and with a pretty oriel window. They were built at the beginning of the 17th century and were timber framed with brick infilling. Originally seven cottages, they were modernised in 1963 and converted into two houses. Much of the exterior has been covered with roughcast. There are more houses and cottages further along by the canal, mainly of the 19th century.

Before returning to the town, note the swing bridge giving access to modern houses on the site of the West Mills watermill, and to a few older properties. On the left when approaching the church are flats on the site of the large Town Mills. Just inside the gates of the church, to the left, is a large flat stone. This was brought from Cheap Street in the early 1970s when buildings there were demolished. It is believed to be the 'bench' on which a medieval bow-string maker rolled strings for archers to use on their long bows. A bow-string maker is recorded as living in that part of the town (see *Transactions of Newbury Field Club*, vol vii, p 84).

ST NICOLAS' CHURCH

St Nicolas' church is a large Tudor building completed around 1530 and believed to have resulted from the generosity of cloth merchants such as Jack of Newbury. The castellations at roof level and pinnacles to the tower are Victorian additions. See also page 36. When leaving the church look at the two stone entrance gateways to the churchyard. These have a Gothic form and decoration and are believed to have been built in 1770.

BARTHOLOMEW STREET

Opposite to the churchyard are a group of late 18th and early 19th century buildings. Further south, the Snooty Fox (formerly The Globe) is a confident pub building of 1875. It incorporates several elements of local traditional building styles – brick-built, tiled roof with prominent bargeboards and decorated with tile-hanging, pilasters and an obvious cornice etc. Sadly, the effect of some of these has been lost through repairs in the past 25 years, especially replacement of the local red tiles of the second floor and painting of the ground floor bricks, breaking the building's unity. Many of the old buildings at the northern end of the street were demolished in the late 1960s and early 1970s, but a few remain. On the west side is another Victorian or Edwardian building, with mock timber framing to the second floor; note the dragon finials at the ends of the roof-ridge, made of terracotta.

The Rat and Parrot (formerly Bricklayer's Arms) has an early 19th century first floor, but the ground floor is much altered, including turning the wagon entrance into a room. Similarly, on the west side, the 18th/19th century buildings occupied by the Citizen's Advice Bureau and Sovereign Housing Association have rebuilt ground floors.

On the west side, number 28 (Charles Lucas and Marshall) is a good early to mid 18th century building, much restored. It has a pretty doorway and fanlight. Three or four years ago CL&M extended into the adjoining building which has a Gothic cornice.

At the south side of Market Street turn off to the east (left) and divert into Inch's Yard (the name from the former Inch's drapery shop on the site). The Madagascan Gin Palace is converted from an 18th century maltings, of which Newbury once had several. Two original mullioned windows (which would have been unglazed) survive, though the two lower ones are replacements. A better impression of this building can be obtained from the rear, by the entrance to the Dolphin's car park. Next to it is a three storey industrial building, the uprights from sets of wooden louvres which once formed the walls of the third floor and two first floor loading doors can be seen, though the brick structure of the building is much altered.

Back on Bartholomew Street, the Dolphin Inn appears to be 17th century and, at the rear, timber framing and tile-hung gables can be seen. The front was rebuilt in the late 18th/early 19th century and has a very flat eliptical arch of rubbed bricks over the former waggon entrance. This entrance, unlike most others, has not been incorporated into the inn, though a large conservatory has been built in the yard. On the opposite side is the Coopers Arms, which appears 18th century, but the interior betrays a 17th century core.

On the east side, the Old Eight Bells (Caffe Soir) was a 16th century inn, as can be seen from the interior, but it was refronted in the 19th century incorporating Gothic windows.

Returning to the west side, Phoenix House (James & Cowper) is a handsome early to mid 18th century house of two storeys and attic with a high parapet. The doorcase and large paned windows are 19th century. For about a century this was the brewer's house and office of the Phoenix Brewery, the 19th century brewery buildings (converted to offices) are to the rear.

Immediately adjacent to the railway bridge (rebuilt 2000), number 61 is a property which was once the Vine Inn (Simply Perfect Nail Studio), thought to date from the 17th century. Restoration of this building and cottages to the rear has only recently been completed, having been carried out gradually over the past ten years; the cottages were in a derelict state. Until a new route was made next to the railway, access to the cottages, dating from the 17th/18th century, immediately behind the former inn, was via a passageway through the Vine.

Across the railway was another inn, The Blackboys Hotel; its painted sign can still be made out on the front of the building. This and the next building (Bartholomew House) which goes round the corner into Pound Street, form one three storey building, dating from the late 18th century and built of red brick. Across the road is a small house and shop (Hugh Stevens, optician) which appears to be timber framed and likely to date from the 17th century. Further along the street, numbers 72 and 73 are a pair of early 19th century houses, stuccoed to emphasise their plain fronts.

POUND STREET and ENBORNE ROAD

The first house on the north side of the street has been converted into a shop but the richly moulded brick cornice and tile-hung gable probably dating from the 17th century are worth attention. The cottages opposite are described under Argyle Road. Further along the south side is a terrace of eight houses built from vitrified grey bricks, mostly used end-on and therefore termed 'headers'. Dark mortar is used with a narrow band of white (called 'tuck pointing') to emphasise the regularity of the brickwork. They are of two storeys with attics in the mansard slate roof. They were probably built in the early 19th century, but could be a little earlier. They form a handsome group and retain most of their original detailing.

Further along, the street becomes Enborne Road; at this point is the former St Nicolas School. This was to the design of William Butterfield, the Victorian architect of so many churches and colleges, and built in 1859. It is very Gothic in its steep roofs and pointed dormers, together with the stepped buttresses. About a quarter of a mile further on is the St Bartholomew's School building of 1885, by Power & Hughes. The main block is Tudor influenced and almost symmetrical.

Return to the end of the street and look at the house almost hidden by a high hedge; this will be described in –

NEWTOWN ROAD

The tall house (Dunwoody Sports Marketing) was built in 1849 as the Grammar School, whilst the flint building adjoining is the remaining section of the 15th century Litten Chapel. Together they now form a set of offices. The chapel originally served St Bartholomew's Hospital (see page 24). Original stone windows can be seen, but its real glory lies in the carved timber roof trusses inside. The east end has been shortened at some time (probably late in the 18th century) as it has been rebuilt in brick. The very high hedge now makes it difficult to see the north elevation.

On the west side of the road and set at right angles to it, are Raymonds' Almshouses. This range of twelve units has a central pedimented entrance way bearing the date 1796. The buildings have been modernised from time to time, introducing several new features. They are known as Lower Raymonds' to differentiate them from a later range (see Derby Road) and replaced the original almshouses in Argyle Road.

Before St John's church is reached, there are two early 19th century houses, probably built 1820/30. Number 24 (LDRA Ltd) is of two storeys in grey brick, used as headers, the door set in a segmental headed stucco recess. The northerly section (No 22) is in a similar style and appears as if it was built as an extension, but has been given its own front door.

St John's church was completed in 1957, replacing the building destroyed in 1943. It was designed by Mr S.E. Dykes-Bower (architect to Westminster Abbey and a well-known church designer) who specified locally-made bricks to non-standard dimensions. Much of the interior is unrendered brick and the quality of the brickwork and vaulting has been admired. In 1988, the church was amongst the first post-1939 buildings to be listed as being of architectural interest.

Newtown Road continues beyond the roundabout, Church and Childs Almshouses are on the left and there are a number of early and later 19th century houses along it, also some in Porchester Road and Priory Road, which lead from it.

ANDOVER ROAD (AND WASH COMMON)

From the roundabout, about five hundred yards along, on the left, opposite to Buckingham Road, is a terrace of four late 18th century cottages, the two end ones being larger buildings. They are of two storeys, under a hipped slate roof; originally the slates would all have been of larger dimensions than those of the 19th and 20th centuries. The doors have ornamental fanlights and are set within an iron trellis porch. On the opposite side is the part of St Bartholomew's School which was built as the Girl's High School in 1909.

Most of the houses in Andover Road and the roads leading off it are of the 20th century, though a few are a little earlier. There are one or two interesting buildings of around 1930 in Tydehams, though changes have been made to the original designs.

Once at Wash Common, Park House School is based around a house of the final decades of the 19th century. Nearby, St George's church is set back from the road. This is an interesting building with an Italian feel to its design. The architect F.C. Eden designed it and the first section was completed in 1933. The western end, tower, 'cloister' and vicarage were designed following the same style, by John Griffin, a local architect, and completed in 1965.

Returning to the roundabout by St John's church, turn west along –

DERBY ROAD

Almost parallel to the north side Upper Raymonds' Almshouses can be seen, though they are entered from Argyle Road. This is a range of ten almshouses built in 1826 in Gothic style. There is a centrepiece of a pointed

Newbury in 2001, with Donnington Castle top left. This vista, from Friars Road, is now one of the very few overviews possible from the south. See also page 88.

stone arch which originally was open through the building. The design of this seems to owe something to the entrances arches of St Nicolas' churchyard.

ARGYLE ROAD

Opposite to Derby Road are the New Nurses Homes, built in 1937 by Dr Essex Wynter for retired nurses of the Middlesex Hospital, London.

To the north are the former Raymonds' Almshouses thought to have been converted from former farm buildings in 1670 by Philip Jemmet, a member of the Brewers Company, hence the company's arms and an appropriate date and initials above the entrance. The almshouses were further endowed by his son-in-law and daughter, Sir Jonathan and Lady Raymond, whose name then became attached to the charity. In the 1920s Dr Essex Wynter purchased the building and altered it by raising the roof on a timber framed structure (confusingly using old materials) to create a second floor for his nurses' home, completed in 1929.

Opposite are St Bartholomew's (sometimes called King John's)

183

Almshouses; its history is outlined on page 24. This most attractive building was erected in 1618, with the entrance tower added in 1698. The Royal Arms are those of the Hanoverian monarchs and therefore 18th century. To the north is the Litten, described under Newtown Road.

Opposite is Bartholomew Manor, so called by Dr Essex Wynter after he restored it as his home (again using old materials) in the 1920s. The house has medieval origins and may date from the 14th or 15th centuries, but has been considerably altered. For many years it was a farmhouse.

To the north and on the corner of Pound Street is another group of old cottages converted by Dr Essex Wynter to provide nurses' accommodation. Though essentially 17th or 18th century single storey cottages with attics they have had substantial renovation, for example there were shop windows in the Argyle Road elevation at the beginning of the 20th century.

Further Reading

Many books have been written on aspects of Newbury's history, its churches and buildings, but few are currently in print. In the list below, those which can currently be purchased are marked **. All of these books and many other can be referred to in Newbury Library and copies of some may be available for loan. Out of print books are often available from rare and secondhand booksellers. Whilst new books are available from most bookshops, the Museum/Tourist Information Centre bookshop at the Wharf aims to sell all local books.

General Histories
The History of Newbury, Walter Money, published 1887.
The Popular History of Newbury, Walter Money, published 1905.
    Reprinted 1972, with foreword by Helen Purvis.
Newbury Scrapbook, Vera F.M. Garlick, published 1970.
Newbury History and Guide, Susan Tolman, published 1994.

It should be noted that, particularly in relation to the older books, more recent research will have changed the interpretation of some information or uncovered new facts.

Illustrated Histories, 19th/20th centuries
Newbury a Photographic Record 1850–1935, Sue Hopson, published
    1983. Reprinted with amendments, 1995.
**Newbury Then and Now, Sue Hopson, published 1988.
Britain in Old Photographs: Newbury, Peter Allen, published 1995.

Old Ordnance Survey Maps
The Godfrey Edition. Reduced scale reprints of maps with accounts of
    the areas covered, concentrating on the period of the map but put in
    an historical context.
**Newbury 1898, 1:2500 scale, Alan Godfrey Maps, published 2000.
**SW Berkshire 1889, 1 inch, Alan Godfrey Maps, published 1999.

Specific Topics
The First and Second Battles of Newbury and the Siege of Donnington
    Castle, Walter Money, published 1881.

This book is of most interest for the contemporary reports it reprints and potted biographies of some contestants. Money's account of the fighting does not concur with modern views. There are many books on the civil wars which contain sections on the battles at Newbury. The small number of contemporary reports of the battles and confusion of those writing, together with the usually partisan approach of their reports, make it impossible to give a categoric account of what happened.

**Shaw House Unmask'd, Michael Macleod, published 1999.

The Great Road to Bath, Daphne Phillips, published 1983.

**A Catalogue of Strolling Companies, the ongoing theatre in Newbury, Paul Ranger, published 1990.

The Bombing of Newbury, Bryan Philpott, published 1989.

The Kennet and Avon Canal, Kenneth Clew (several editions).

**Working Waterway, The Kennet & Avon Canal Through West Berkshire, West Berkshire Heritage Service, 1999.

Newbury Buildings Past and Present, H.H. Coghlan, published 1973.

**Articles on a variety of local historical and archaeological topics in The Transactions of Newbury District Field Club, published from 1872 to present.

Index